THE HEALING PATH

A 30-Day Devotional to Help You Cross the Bridge from Hurting to Healing

KATIE FILIATREAU

Lightkeeper Books
Nashville, Tennessee

LIGHTKEEPER

BOOKS

LIGHTKEEPER
BOOKS

TABLE OF CONTENTS

If the Bible is a roadmap meant to guide us, Katie leads those of us in search of healing down the right path. It's a path she's spent the last several years navigating on a personal and professional level, so she's well versed in the twists and turns and ups and downs of it. The destination is wholeness, and in this book, you'll be handed some simple tools that will help you get from where you are to where you most want to be. Pace yourself and be patient with yourself on this journey. And remember along the way, that whatever nagging pain you've learned to live with over the years, you'll be glad you finally took the steps to get better.

—**Jon Weece**, Lead Pastor, Southland Christian Church

PREFACE

If you would like to dig deeper through this journey, I've created a companion resource to help you. You can download your free *The Healing Path Journal* by going to katiefiliatreau.com.

Just like I walk my patients through their physical healing—from assessing their pain to tracking their progress—this journal will give you a template to help you on your heart healing journey.

You'll find reflection questions plus more exercises to help you find your pain points and track the ways God shows up for you along your journey.

Go to katiefiliatreau.com to download your free copy.

HURTING - THE JOURNEY STARTS HERE

I walked through the door and set my keys on the counter. It had been a long week. I had been ignoring an old, nagging pain in my lower back, and it was shouting at me again. I pulled out an ice pack and rested through the weekend.

When my pain was still aggravated on Monday morning, I decided to ask for help from a co-worker at the physical therapy clinic where I work. There is a quick stretch that always helps. It's at least effective enough to relieve my symptoms so I can manage the pain and get through the day.

My pain follows a pattern: symptoms flare, my colleague helps me stretch, I get just enough relief to keep me from addressing the root cause, but then the pain pops back up. This time, my co-worker didn't just do the stretch and let me go. He challenged me to stop taking the easy route for pain relief, and he walked me through the steps of the healing process.

It was a hard truth to face. After all, I should know better. I've spent my entire professional career as a physical therapist. I see pain every day—back pain, neck pain, shoulder pain. We all have pain, and we manage it independently, often for too long. We ignore the problem, take medication, and avoid activities. Eventually, we realize the pain isn't going away, so we seek guidance.

When patients finally walk through my clinic doors, they are worn out, weary, and desperate to ease the pain. The best part of my job is getting to tell them the good news: "You don't have to be in pain forever. We will figure out the cause and take steps toward relief. It will require discipline and trust. But there is hope, and you can find freedom from pain at the end of the healing path."

Physical therapy helps us heal from physical pain. Shouldn't there be a similar process to address the pain in our hearts and souls? Anxiety. Fear. Loneliness. People-pleasing. Perfectionism. We all struggle with pain points of the heart and soul—symptoms of a deeper issue that desperately need to be addressed.

Oh, Jesus, how true that statement is in my life emotionally and spiritually as well!

When we seek a quick fix, it may supply some short-term relief, but none of it is what we actually need for healing.

We are gradually overcoming the stigma associated with seeking counsel to address our mental and emotional health. According to the CDC, 20.3% of US adults received any mental health treatment in 2020. These numbers continue to trend upward as confirmed by a 2021 article from the American Psychological Association: The number of psychologists who reported receiving more referrals in 2021 almost doubled from those this year before, from 37% to 62%.

It is clear that we are hurting, and we are desperate for healing. The question remains: how do we get there?

This is not a multiple-choice question with only one right answer. It is a journey. But with a good roadmap and the right tools, you can get there. My prayer is that you'll come with an open heart and consider stepping into a transformational experience where Jesus will meet you exactly where you are.

Whether it's physical or emotional wounds that leave us in pain, it's easy to seek a short-term fix. I must confess, I've been there. Yet, Jesus wants so much more for us all—He wants to be our long-term solution.

How do I know Jesus cares? Because he said so himself in Mark 2:17. When the religious leaders saw Jesus spending time with people who didn't have it all together, they criticized him. But Jesus's response was clear: *"When*

Jesus heard this, he told them, 'Healthy people don't need a doctor—sick people do.'"

When I finally made the decision to begin addressing my emotional pain in the same way I know how to resolve physical pain, I stepped into a journey of healing my heart and soul. Taking the first step was difficult, and my path was filled with hills and valleys. Often, I had no idea what was around the next corner, but Jesus always provided enough light to take the next step. It was the hardest and best thing I've ever done.

Bridging the Gap

I would love for you to experience the transformational and healing love of Jesus. This book supplies a roadmap for your journey. Each section will lead you and provide encouragement as you move through the steps from hurting to healing.

Before we dive deeper, let's look at what this path looks like.

Step 1: Hope

When we're hurting, our vision is affected. It's difficult to see what lies ahead and that halts our ability to move forward. Hebrews 11:1 says, *"Faith shows the reality of what we hope for; it is the evidence of things we cannot see."*

Hope helps us begin our journey, and it is what we must cling to in order to take the first steps toward healing:

- Recognizing our hurt
- Identifying the symptoms
- Deciding to seek healing

Step 2: Discipline

When we are walking down a path of healing, suffering is inevitable. If we try to avoid it, we often never reach our destination. When we begin to see the pain as productive, we can choose to continue walking the path with discipline.

Romans 5:3–4 says: *"We can rejoice, too, when we run into problems and trials, for we know that they help us develop endurance. And endurance develops strength of character, and character strengthens our confident hope of salvation."*

During this stage, we'll talk about tools that will help you push through the adversity and reach your destination of healing:

- Reading the Bible and prayer
- Mentorship and support from trusted friends
- Professional counseling

Step 3: Trust

As we travel the narrow path of our journey of spiritual and emotional healing, we are constantly faced with a decision. Do we try to navigate the process on our own, or will we choose to trust Jesus with the unknown? Psalm 55:22 asks us to let go and trust: *"Give your burdens to the Lord, and he will take care of you. He will not permit the godly to slip and fall."*

When the road seems long, Jesus will guide you. If He can do it for me, you can trust him to do it for you. During this stage, we will lean into three skills:

- Commitment to change
- Mindfulness
- Identifying God's faithfulness

Stepping Forward

Each of these three steps include ten days of devotions designed to offer courage and support as you step into your healing process.

I have more freedom and joy in my life today because of God's healing power. I would love for you to experience the same. But you don't have to take the journey alone.

Over the course of the next three chapters, I will share glimpses of my story, offer perspective from the process of physical healing, and uncover the love Jesus wants to give each of us.

When we begin to think of our emotional wounds in the same way we think about a cut we get from the playground or a sore back from working in the yard, we can begin to bridge the gap from hurting to healing our hearts.

Hope. Discipline. Trust. These three steps are the bridge that answers the question: *How do I get from hurting to healing?*

Let's take the first step together.

The Healing Path Journal

If you would like to dig deeper through this journey, I've created a companion resource to help you. You can download your free Healing Path Journal at katiefiliatreau.com.

Just like I walk my patients through their physical healing—from assessing their pain to tracking their progress—this journal will give you a template to help you on your heart healing journey.

You'll find reflection questions plus more exercises to help you name your pain points and track the ways God shows up for you along your journey.

Download your free copy by going to katiefiliatreau.com.

Reflection Questions

1. Answer these three questions with a simple yes or no.

   - Do you find yourself constantly feeling a sense of unsettledness or discontent?
   - Is there a hurt in your heart or soul that you've been ignoring for a long time, hoping it would just go away?
   - Do you find yourself wanting to feel better (more hopeful, peaceful, joyful, etc.) but just don't know where to start to get there?

2. Are there specific areas in your life where you'd like to see healing? What would healing look like (E.g., a stronger relationship with your kids? Mend or grow your relationship with a friend or family member? Joy and peace instead of anxiety? Confidence in your unique identity?)

STEP 1 – HOPE

Have you ever continued to do something the same way even though it's painful? For example, it hurts your back to get into and out of the car, but you put up with it. It hurts your shoulder to toss a ball with your kid, but you ignore the pain. It hurts your neck when you work on your computer, but you still do it.

We often travel down a path of pain simply because we are unaware there is a better way. Once we begin to recognize our struggles and name our pain points, we can choose to change course and move in a direction that will lead us to experience less pain and more freedom.

I see this daily in my work. Patients show up for their first visit only after they've recognized there is a problem. It is then my job as their physical therapist to help them dive deeper into the process of finding the root cause of their symptoms.

We talk about what makes their symptoms worse and what makes them better. We talk about the quality and quantity of their pain. It's only when they can recognize and express their symptoms that I can begin walking with them down a healing path of doing things differently.

We might change their lifting technique. We may change the way they throw a ball. We could alter their posture while they're sitting at their desk.

Many times, the patient has been dealing with their pain for a long time. That means the change will be hard—it's not easy to replace old habits. Creating new muscle memory takes time, but the outcome of the process is an easing of the pain.

The same is true when we begin to recognize the pain we're carrying in our hearts and souls. We first must identify our symptoms, then decide to seek healing.

Recognize the Hurts

Every experience we have in life directs our path. At some point on the journey, we must make a choice. Instead of continuing to manage symptoms that are an indicator of deeper wounds we've chosen to ignore, we must begin to recognize the hurts that are holding us captive.

I grew up in a small town as the only sister to three brothers, the youngest of which is my twin. I was highly motivated by achievement. I wanted to ace every test, win every game, and earn a scholarship to college. I was determined to get into physical therapy school and perform at the top of my class so employers would want to hire me.

I was striving to achieve so I could fill an emptiness in my heart as our family had some difficult dynamics. But with every achievement, I was left with the realization that the victories and test scores were never enough.

As someone who has always been relationship-oriented, my desire to connect with people, learn more about them, and develop deep connections has been a consistent driver in my life. While some relationships have blessed me with strong friendships spanning a variety of generations and demographics, others have been challenging and painful.

I was a good person, I was successful, and I had a lot of friends. I went to church. I believed in God. Yet I found myself continuing to struggle with loneliness, feeling unfulfilled, and seeking something more.

In 2016, a friend gently invited me to attend a women's conference with her. I was nervous and hesitant. Events like this were out of my comfort zone. But I finally said yes.

Up to that point I knew about God, I even talked to Him in prayer. But the steps of my life continued to be marked more by the pain in my heart and less by the loving God who created me.

That conference was unlike anything I had ever experienced. There, I learned the difference between going to church and following Jesus. And I made a choice to move from faith being a mere cog in the wheel of my life to my relationship with Jesus driving everything.

I began to look for God's plan and purpose for my life. It was my first step onto the healing path.

Identify the Symptoms

Just like on any journey, my new life with Jesus was just the beginning. I had a relationship with the great Healer, but I still had to tend to the wounds of my heart.

God has a way of using people in our lives to get our attention. I still remember the day a close friend had the courage to have a difficult conversation with me. Many words and tears later, I started to realize just how much my heart was hurting.

As I processed our conversation, I began to ask Jesus to help me identify the symptoms of my hurting heart. An identity problem, fear, and people-pleasing were just a few of the pain points that marked the path I had been walking for years.

My life hasn't been all pain or all joy—it's simply both. This is true for every single one of us. Our lives are marked by good, bad, and ugly. When we pause to reflect on our individual perspectives, we can begin to see how they have shaped our journey.

The beautiful truth is the hard and pain do not have to define us. They can, however, be what motivates us to look for a more peaceful and joy-filled life.

Decide to Seek Healing

As I was struggling to find direction, the Lord reminded me it is through faith in Jesus that I could take the first step on my journey from hurting to healing.

According to John 14:6, Jesus said, *"I am the way, and the truth, and the life. No one comes to the Father except through me."*

This verse is often used to remind us that faith in Jesus is how we are assured of an eternity in heaven. While that is true, Jesus also cares about our "truth and life" while we are here on earth. He showed this through His miracles of bringing healing. He even told the religious leaders he was on earth to heal the sick. (Remember what Jesus said in Mark 2:17? *Healthy people don't need a doctor—sick people do.*)

When I began to understand that Jesus was the true starting point to healing, I found the courage to place my trust in His healing plan - both for eternity and in my daily life here on earth. And I chose to follow this plan, even if it required me to do things in ways I had never done before.

If you are willing, this book can help you begin to step into this process for yourself. As you recognize a need, begin to name the pain points of your heart and soul. Commit to the process.

As a physical therapist, I ask my patients to do specific exercises at home. The work they do between sessions is a critical part of their physical healing. The same is true for emotional and spiritual healing. So, I'm going to ask you to do a little homework, too.

Over the next ten days, commit to setting aside 10–15 minutes each day—in the early morning, on your lunch break, or before bed, whatever works best for you—then read one of the devotional passages that follow. (If you'd like to take your study even deeper, be sure to download your free companion journal at katiefiliatreau.com.)

Each day's devotion will walk you through ways that Jesus shows up in our everyday life and will encourage you to lean into the hope found in Him. Jesus will provide the guidance you need as you discover that, with Him, there is always a better way.

Take the first step today.

Reflection Questions

1. Think about the path your life has taken. What are at least three unique experiences that have shaped your life? In just five minutes, write down as many as you can think of. This will help you begin the process of identifying symptoms.

2. Have you been wounded? Write down examples that come to mind. Be as specific as possible. Who or what hurt you? How did it make you feel? Are those wounds showing up in your life today? How?

3. Do you recognize any symptoms of pain in your heart? Fear, anxiety, striving for achievement, loneliness, using food or substances for comfort, shame, anger, or depression. Take two to three minutes and write down any that come to mind.

Day 1: Weary Traveler

Good news from far away is like cold water to the thirsty.

Proverbs 25:25

Being an aunt to ten nieces and nephews is one of the greatest joys of my life. So much so that I will often choose to spend my free time, extra money, paid time off, with or directly on them. My love for them runs deep. I can't imagine the depth of love a parent has for their children, much less the depth of love Jesus has for you and me.

One New Year's weekend, I volunteered to help my mom watch three of these blessings. At the time, they were six months, five years, and almost seven. They are wonderful kids and so well-behaved. But as you may know, kids demand a lot of attention.

We put together puzzles, played games, circled countless hidden objects, changed diapers, made bottles, picked up toys, put them down for naps, and carried the baby around on repeat, for several days in a row.

Three full days and two long nights later, I returned to the quiet of my home. A hot shower and a nap were calling my name—luxuries most parents of young kids would die for. But then my brother called. Their flight had been canceled. So, I hopped back in the car and drove the hour back to help my mom for one more night.

I called a friend during the drive. Knowing I was feeling tired (and a little grumpy), she suggested I listen to some worship music to reposition my heart. She laughed at my apathetic response, but we both knew she was right.

It is usually when we *need* to pray and worship that we feel least like doing so. As I approached the house, nearing the end of my hour drive, I turned up the radio to hear these lyrics from the song "Weary Traveler" by Jordan St. Cyr:

Weary traveler, restless soul

You were never meant to walk this road alone

It'll all be worth it so just hold on

Weary traveler, you won't be weary long

The words landed on my heart with perfect timing and reminded me that no matter how worn out and weary we may feel, we are never alone. The best news of all is that when we choose to place our hope and faith in Jesus, we won't be weary long.

You may be carrying burdens and fighting battles, and each day, you may just be trying to put one foot in front of the other. As followers of Jesus, because this world is not our home, we all are weary travelers.

But Proverbs 25:25 says: *"Good news from far away is like cold water to the thirsty."* The best news of all is that when we speak with our mouths and believe in our hearts that Jesus Christ is Lord, we are saved by faith through grace from all our sins for all of eternity (Romans 10:9). Being saved is a gift to our weary souls, and it restores our once-broken relationship with God. That truth, if we allow it to sink into our hearts, will always be enough to help us hold on.

Take 5: I love worship music. It has a way of centering our soul in the strength and love of Jesus. Take five minutes and listen to a favorite worship song. Use the lyrics to praise God for who He is. Thank Him for being with you today.

Day 2: Following Where He Leads

I know, Lord, that our lives are not our own. We are not able to plan our own course.

Jeremiah 10:23

I sometimes like watching *Let's Make a Deal*. The prizes are hidden behind door number one, two, or three, and contestants must choose a door while not knowing what they would find behind each of them. This creates a suspenseful game where contestants are sometimes left disappointed, but they also lean into the hope of the prize value increasing dramatically when they select the "right" door.

Several things could affect the choice the contestant makes—their favorite number, the roar of the crowd, and sometimes just following their heart. This makes for a fun way to play a game show, but it certainly is not how we make important choices in our daily lives.

Every day, we are faced with making decisions. Some are simple; others may be weighty.

What should I wear to work?

What should I cook for supper?

Where should I apply for college?

Should I move my family for a new job?

We are surrounded by so much noise affecting our decisions. Before we know it, we feel overwhelmed and fall into the trap of allowing external factors to carry greater weight in our decision-making than how the Lord is prompting us to move.

As a physical therapist, I have the opportunity to affect the lives of my patients every day. My hope is always to help them with their physical ailments and empower them to return to living a better quality of life. I love my job, but I don't want to limit the ways God can use me. Every day, I choose to pause and ask the Lord to guide my steps.

Choosing "door one" might hold access to my medical skills as a physical therapist. Behind "door two" may be a gift of words that the Lord can use to speak truth. And "door three" might lead me to step into a role of service within my local community. There are lots of things trying to change which door I choose. That's why I am thankful for the truth in Jeremiah 10:23: *"I know, Lord, that our lives are not our own. We are not able to plan our own course."*

Just like *Let's Make a Deal*, we don't fully know what is behind each of the doors in front of us. However, if we choose to trust the Lord to be our guide, we can be disciplined to step through every door He leads us to. I am a physical therapist. I am a writer. I am a serving member of my community.

May you ask yourself today if you have limited your kingdom contribution by telling yourself you can only choose door one, two, or three. As followers of Christ, we don't have to limit ourselves, and we certainly don't have to heed the direction of the crowd. By choosing discipline and trust, we can follow Jesus wherever He leads. And we can be confident He will use our choice for our good and His glory.

Take 5: Take a few moments to consider areas where God may be inviting you. Is it a place to serve a place to heal? Or both? Thank Him for the love that gives you the courage to step out in hope and faith.

Day 3: Routine Maintenance

Look after each other so that none of you fails to receive the grace of God. Watch out that no poisonous root of bitterness grows up to trouble you, corrupting many.

Hebrews 12:15

As a physical therapist working at multiple sites, my workday is typically scheduled down to the minute. One morning, I found myself rushing out the door and peeling out of the parking lot to my next destination where patients were already waiting.

It was twenty-nine degrees out, so I reached forward to turn on the heat. I was blasted with more terribly cold air. *I am really going to have to get this car looked at soon,* I thought. Then, I noticed the temperature gauge going up. Yet another sign something was definitely wrong with my car.

I quickly pulled over to check under the hood. had been dealing with a small leak in the radiator, and though I had topped off the coolant the day before, the tank was nearly empty. I now had a much bigger problem on my hands. Unless I addressed it, I could risk blowing the radiator!

The Lord had taken care of me that day—I had taken a different route than I normally do, so I was just a mile from a friend's house. I cautiously drove to my friend's home, and she graciously gave me a ride to my destination. The goodness of God showed up through faithful friends that helped me get through the day while I waited for my car to be repaired.

As I reflected on the events of the day, I felt the Lord ask me: *Have you done any routine maintenance on your heart lately?*

Just like our vehicles, our hearts can develop slow leaks over time that, if left unaddressed, can wreak havoc in our lives. Hebrews 12:15 says: *"Look after each other so that none of you fails to receive the grace of God. Watch out that no poisonous root of bitterness grows up to trouble you, corrupting many."*

Sometimes, I neglect to realize how my unchecked negative emotions can affect those around me in a hurtful way.

Just as our vehicles have gauges to help us know when we have a problem, we must surround ourselves with friends who are willing to be a gauge for us. We need friends who will gently and lovingly hold us accountable when they notice a leak. I am so grateful for godly friends in my life that help me recognize any "emotional leaks" before they turn into a huge problem.

This list of analogies helps us to examine our hearts in the same way we examine our vehicles:

Owner's manual = God's Word

Temperature gauge = Godly friends

Under the hood = Into our hearts

Mechanic = Jesus

What do we do with those warning signs? We turn to Jesus, the ultimate mechanic. We open our hearts, give Him an opportunity to look around, and let Him show us the areas that need to be addressed.

It might be scary at first—it often is when we don't know what we will find. Like any repair, it may come at a cost—especially when we've ignored the warning lights for too long. But I promise you, giving Jesus full access to our hearts is always worth it. In Him, we find hope for repair.

Take 5: Ask Jesus to help you open your heart to Him and find what needs repair. Thank Him for being the healer of your heart.

Day 4: The Curves of Life

Teach these new disciples to obey all the commands I have given you. And be sure of this: I am with you always, even to the end of the age.

Matthew 28:20

As a physical therapist, I often work with young athletes. I love it, because it combines three things I'm passionate about: physical therapy, sports, and engaging with young adults.

I once asked one of my baseball players about the different pitches he throws. He rattled off a few, but said his favorite is the curveball. When I asked him why, he said, "I love watching the guys at the plate freeze. They're expecting a different pitch, the ball hangs up, dives at the last second, and their bat catches the air."

Talented players make hitting a baseball look easy, but I assure you it's not. The more years you play the game, the challenge only increases in complexity and difficulty. At first, it's just fastballs you worry about. But then come the two-seam fastball, four-seam fastball, curve, slider, and change-up. So even if you learn to be an excellent fastball hitter, if you can't learn to adjust to off-speed pitches like the curve, it's going to be difficult to be successful at the higher levels of play.

Isn't life often like that, too? We get used to the fastball routine of life. Most days, we run through the same motions of waking up, getting ready, going to school or work, and then coming home to take care of whatever chores await us. But when curves of life are thrown our way—an illness, a layoff, an unexpected natural disaster—we often aren't ready for it.

A good friend once told me, "Life only gets harder. The more time you spend growing in your relationship with Christ, the more equipped you'll be to face the curves of life." That was nearly ten years ago. And he was right.

It's not always fastballs right down the pipe anymore. As we progress into adulthood, we step up to the plate and are often challenged with facing the curves of life: financial hardships, sickness, infertility, broken relationships, and so many other things are bearing down on us daily.

Though life is hard, we have the promises of God, like the one from Matthew 28:20 to lean on: *"Teach these new disciples to obey all the commands I have given you. And be sure of this: I am with you always, even to the end of the age."*

The Lord has provided for me in so many ways, and he continues to do so. Through a lot of prayer, tears, and countless hours of counseling, my relationship with Jesus has grown tremendously over the last several years.

I no longer step into the batter's box of life expecting to see only fastballs. Because of my growing relationship with Jesus, I am more equipped when it comes to facing the curves of life. Even if I don't hit every curveball that's thrown my way, I remember Jesus's promise that He is always with me in the batter's box of life. He promises the same thing for you, too.

Take 5: Taking the first steps on the healing path is not easy. Take five minutes to write out the verse for today and fill your mind with God's promise to be with you always. Put it in a note on your phone, tape it to your mirror, or slip it in your planner. Read it again and stand on His promise.

Day 5: The Attic of Our Souls

This means that anyone who belongs to Christ has become a new person. The old life is gone; a new life has begun!

2 Corinthians 5:17

One morning, I noticed spots along one wall in my kitchen where the paint was cracking. After sending a few pictures to a friend, he confirmed my suspicion. "Looks like you've got a leak somewhere." He assured me he would check things out in a few days, so I pushed my worry aside.

My friend showed up as promised, and we discovered that a piece of vinyl siding had blown off. After some repairs, I felt confident my problem was solved. A few days later, I began hearing a drip, drip, drip. I went to my kitchen to find water dripping from the ceiling!

After a few phone calls with knowledgeable friends, I checked other areas of my house. I even climbed the stairs to the attic, where yet again, I heard a drip, drip, drip.

Fast-forward two months, I had a new roof. Though it was a tumultuous and costly process, I am so thankful for the Lord's provision of financial security, friends who provided comfort and support, and an entire week of no rain during installation.

My new roof provided a significant sense of relief, as I knew my home would be protected from further damage and drips. But even so, I caught myself worrying about the potential for new leaks in the attic.

"Lord, I don't want to go up there," I prayed. "What if I find more leaks, even after the new roof, then what do I do? I think it's better if I just don't look."

The Lord reminded me that the situation with my attic was much like the spiritual healing of my soul. Some days I just don't want to look at the mess. It's easier to ignore the problems I know are there, but once I take the first step of examination, that's when the process of cleanup and healing truly begins.

I remember the first day I went to counseling. Though I knew it was a safe place, it didn't alleviate the fear of the unknown. Without courage and strength from the Lord, I never would have walked into my counselor's office that day.

What I didn't realize was that I would be starting a journey of spiritual healing that would change my life. Once I finally decided to check for leaks in the attic of my soul, the Lord began to work in my life in ways I never could have imagined.

Had I left the leaks in my house unchecked, they would have caused major damage over time. Similarly, if I continued to ignore the wounded parts of my soul, they would have continued to cause major damage in every part of my life.

The first evening after an all-day rain, I was filled with relief to find the new roof had done its job. But it wasn't because I chose to patch the leaks. Instead, it was because my leaky old roof had been replaced with a new one.

In 2 Corinthians 5:17, we are assured of this truth: *"This means that anyone who belongs to Christ has become a new person. The old life is gone; a new life has begun!"*

When you and I say yes to Jesus and commit to tearing away the old in our hearts, the healing of our souls can begin. The journey isn't easy, but when the contractor for your soul is Jesus, you can begin to walk confidently as He leads you on the path of healing the attic of your soul.

Take 5: Pause and reflect today. Ask Jesus to reveal areas of your heart and soul that maybe you've been choosing to ignore. Write down whatever comes to mind. Tell Jesus what you need and allow Him to lead you.

Day 6: Say Yes!

Such love has no fear because perfect love expels all fear. If we are afraid, it is for fear of punishment, and this shows that we have not fully experienced his perfect love.

1 John 4:18

Michael Jordan is the GOAT—the greatest of all time— when it comes to basketball. While not everyone would agree with my assessment, he's always been my favorite. He is 6'6", and at the height of his career, he could run fast, jump high, and had a silky-smooth jumper.

But that's not the only reason I admire him. I consider him the GOAT not only because of his God-given talents but because of the ways he chose to use those talents. He was the fiercest competitor, hated to lose, gave everything he had, expected that of his teammates, and left everything on the court.

As a freshman in high school, Michael was cut from the team. It's mind-boggling that an individual who faced that type of rejection would go on to become one of the most decorated players in the history of the National Basketball Association. But Michael didn't let fear stop him from pursuing what he loved—another reason I love his story so much.

After Michael was cut, he didn't quit. Instead, he went home and went to work. Despite his past failure, and fear of possibly failing again, he chose to say yes to the challenge. He put in the time and pushed himself harder than anyone else. He practiced and he chose to pursue something God uniquely designed him for: playing the game of basketball.

We've all faced fear and failure in our lives. It's one of the reasons I love the verse from 1 John 4:18 so much: *"Such love has no fear, because perfect love expels all fear. If we are afraid, it is for fear of punishment, and this shows that we have not fully experienced his perfect love."*

This verse was a foundational truth for me as I embarked on my journey of spiritual healing. When I began to feel fear—especially as I found myself during the most challenging season of my life—I could counter the fear by remembering that I am perfectly loved by my Heavenly Father. Once I remembered that truth, I could push past fear and press forward into the future.

I have two stickers on my laptop: the Michael Jordan logo and another that reads, "Say Yes!" These stickers make a good pair because they remind me that when failure and fear mark my journey, I have two choices: I can quit, or I can say yes to holding on to the truth and pushing forward into something I am passionate about.

I have no idea if Michael Jordan knows Jesus, but I can look at his journey and see how the Lord was with him through his failure, fear, and ultimately his final landing place as one of the best to ever play the game of basketball.

In life, when we choose to step out in pursuit of a passion, fear and failure will always be lurking. Still, we can push past those fears when we remember that God perfectly loves us. And whatever the Lord prompts us to do, He will walk through it with us, embracing us with His perfect love.

Take 5: Are there areas of your life where you're allowing fear to hold you back? Pause and consider them today. Share your heart with Jesus and allow His perfect love to guide you to all He has for you.

Day 7: Comfortable with Sin

So now there is no condemnation for those who belong to Christ Jesus.

Romans 8:1

I love my living room furniture. It's stylish, lightweight, and, best of all, super comfortable. I especially love what I call "my Jesus chair." It was a piece I bought long before I purchased my home, when I still lived in a small apartment.

In my chair is where I spend my first quiet moments every morning. It's where I crash in the evenings after a long day of work. I once would have thought it interesting to say that a piece of furniture has been a huge blessing in my life, but it's true. That chair has been such a gift.

If I'm not careful, this gift can easily become a trap. It can also be a place where comfort can keep me stagnant. I can end up spending hours in it watching TV, reading, and scrolling through social media.

While rest is not a bad thing, it can become a destructive thing when it pulls me into complacency, and laziness. Before I know it, I've allowed myself to become comfortable in a way that leads to sin.

There are scriptures in the Bible that talk about laziness, but I don't think they apply strictly to being lazy in the physical sense. When I reflect upon this in a spiritual way, it gives me pause.

What kind of influences am I filling my mind and heart with? What kind of TV am I watching, and what kind of music am I listening to? How much time am I spending on social media, and how is that affecting my heart? Who am I spending my time with, and how are they affecting my representation of Christ?

I am not suggesting that we should live our lives expecting to live every moment perfectly. Sin is an unavoidable part of life. However, when we choose to place our faith in Christ, our hearts undergo a process whereby we grow, heal, and are set apart for a specific purpose designed by God.

But the enemy is deceitful and very deliberate. One of Satan's ultimate goals is to blind us to the truth of God's grace, mercy, and love. He tries to lure us into complacency where we accept things in our lives that we know God doesn't want for us.

Today is an opportunity for us to step back and ponder these questions:

What sins have I allowed myself to become comfortable with?

Where has complacency become the choice over confrontation in the name of Jesus?

How has my decision to "sit in sin" kept me from stepping into the plans God has for my life?

May we be mindful today not to fall into the trap of comfort, which may cause us to settle for less than what God wants for our life and remember the promise from Romans 8:1 that *"there is no condemnation for those who belong to Christ Jesus."*

When we pray and ask God to reveal to our hearts the areas where we've become complacent, we can begin to make decisions to move forward with Jesus rather than still being comfortable in our sin.

Take 5: Use the questions above to take an inventory of your routine and habits. Write down what's become comfortable that you need to confront. Ask the Lord to lead you in confidence, not condemnation, into a future with Jesus.

Day 8: Answering the Call

Now someone may argue, "Some people have faith; others have good deeds." But I say, "How can you show me your faith if you don't have good deeds? I will show you my faith by my good deeds."

James 2:18

I woke up at 5:30 a.m. one Saturday morning. I had no reason to be up early, but I began to feel a nudge in my gut that it was the Lord who had woken me to get up to write. I lay there a few more minutes before responding to the Lord's prompting.

The day before, I had spent many hours staring at my computer screen, struggling with the order and flow of my words. I finally hit pause and asked the Holy Spirit to guide me.

Sometimes when I hit a wall and can't find the words, I sense God wanting me to push through and keep writing. Other times, I want to throw in the towel, or at least step away and come back when I feel refreshed. That is what I had done the night before, and that Saturday morning, God woke me up with a clear mind and the right words.

Learning more about this process and how the Lord works t giving me words has been such a blessing. It saves me from staring at a blank screen and a blinking cursor, but more importantly, it feels like a true partnership between God and me.

Partnering with God in my writing process was a faith builder. As I saw Him give me words for the page, I began to trust Him in other ways. When I sensed an invitation from God to commit myself to more time for writing and spending time with Him, I decreased my hours at work so I could set aside Friday. It wasn't easy—our culture tends to push us to do more, not less. But I've seen the Lord honor this commitment.

Friday has become my favorite day of the week, not only because I don't have to go to work—though that helps—but also because it has become a day where I have more time to sit with the Lord.

Most of the time, He gives me words, and so I write. Other times, He gives me silence, and so I rest. Often, He gives me the opportunity for connection by meeting friends for lunch. God has also blessed me on Fridays with space for growth by meeting with mentors over coffee. Each week, I can't wait to see what the Lord has in store for me.

James 2:14–18 are some of my favorite verses. James asks, *"What good is it, dear brothers and sisters, if you say you have faith but don't show it by your actions? Can that kind of faith save anyone? Suppose you see a brother or sister who has no food or clothing, and you say, 'Good-bye and have a good day; stay warm and eat well'—but then you don't give that person any food or clothing. What good does that do? So, you see, faith by itself isn't enough. Unless it produces good deeds, it is dead and useless. Now someone may argue, 'Some people have faith; others have good deeds.' But I say, 'How can you show me your faith if you don't have good deeds? I will show you my faith by my good deeds.'"*

In simpler terms, faith without action is dead. For the longest time, I had faith that the Lord could, and would, do something big with the words He has put on my heart. However, my faith was put into action when I finally gave the Lord the time He had been asking for.

Is there something the Lord has been asking of you? Do you need to take that training, reach out to a neighbor, or give time to a project on your heart? Take time to consider that today and remember this: when you follow the Lord down the narrow path and answer His invitation, it always leads to life.

Take 5: Is there something the Lord has been asking of you? Take five minutes to journal and write down what He lays on your heart.

Day 9: A Revolving Door

Look! The virgin will conceive a child! She will give birth to a son, and they will call him Immanuel, which means "God is with us."

Matthew 1:23

I've gone on a lot of first dates. Coffee dates. Dinner dates. Walk-in-the-park dates. Ice cream dates. The list is much longer than I ever imagined it would be, and each time it's my hope that it will be my last first date. Though I often end up feeling like I'm stuck in a revolving door, I have promised the Lord throughout this process that I would keep my heart open to whatever He may have for me.

After going on a couple of dates that didn't work out, a friend texted me: "God is trustworthy."

Though her words were few, they were very powerful. If the revolving door of dating has taught me one thing, it is to lean into that truth. Though pangs of disappointment always go with the end of another dating experience, my heart has grown in tremendous ways.

Trust requires faith, and faith, as we are told in Hebrews 11:1, requires us to lean into a confidence that is based on something that we cannot see: *"Now faith is confidence in what we hope for and assurance about what we do not see."*

Through the failures and disappointments of my dating experiences, I have learned so much about the goodness of God. In Him, my identity is rooted. He is my protector. He is my foundation. He is the source of unconditional love.

Admittedly, it's often easier to stand aside and watch the revolving door go around and around. But if I make that choice, what will I miss? Will I miss experiencing the Lord in my life in a way that has taught me so much about His sovereignty.

Is there something in your life that you hope for or need, yet you feel like you're stuck in a continuously revolving door? I'd like to encourage you today. If the Lord is asking you to continue trusting Him with this hope, keep putting one foot in front of the other.

When we choose to keep our eyes fixed on Him even though we may end up stuck longer than expected, may we remember the promise from Matthew 1:23: *"Look! The virgin will conceive a child! She will give birth to a son, and they will call him Immanuel, which means 'God is with us.'"*

Can you imagine how Mary, the mother of Jesus, may have felt throughout the entire experience of learning she was to bear and give birth to the Son of God? Doubt. Unbelief. Fear. Confusion. The emotions had to have been many, but she chose to lean into hope, faith, and trust.

Immanuel, God is with us. When I remember this truth and lean into it, I can continue walking forward in faith toward the desires of my heart, knowing the Lord is with me every single moment. So, each time I step into a new dating experience, I am hopeful. But my assurance is not found in the experience of dating but rather in my Heavenly Father, the One who holds my life in the palm of His hand.

Take 5: Take a few minutes to pause and pray. Allow yourself to exchange the frustration of your revolving door for the freedom that comes from knowing God is with you and has a great plan for your life.

Day 10: Get Up and Go

The Lord had said to Abram, "Leave your native country, your relatives, and your father's family, and go to the land that I will show you."

Genesis 12:1

Where's your favorite place in your home? The place you go when you need some quiet, comfort, and relaxation. It might be your couch, or maybe it's kicked back in your La-Z-Boy. You can often find me nestled in my favorite chair surrounded by everything I need to be comfortable.

I was in my cozy spot one morning chatting with a friend. After sharing with her that I'd injured my arm, my friend began asking all the right questions about what I had done to help with the pain. Truthfully, I hadn't done anything about it because I didn't want to get up. I was too comfortable.

Life is often like that. We choose comfort because it's easy, and it's what we know. Comfort, while a blessing, can also often cause us to struggle. Many times, we choose to suffer simply because we don't want to disrupt our current situation. I had immediate access to something that would help decrease my pain. Yet, I resisted because it would require me to step away from what was comfortable.

Shortly after I committed to giving God specific space to work on my heart through words, I found myself facing a difficult season. During that time, the Lord walked with me through some major challenges and taught me to lean into Him while He healed my hurting heart.

When we say yes to the Lord, we are sometimes met with resistance in our attempt to move forward. Thankfully, Jesus will guide us every step of the way.

I think it's fair for all of us to look at our lives and ask what places we have allowed comfort to become king. Have you felt the Lord calling you into something that is outside your comfort zone? Maybe it's a house you've been thinking about buying or a job you've considered taking. Maybe it's launching a small business or saying yes to becoming a foster parent.

The Lord had been pursuing and pushing me to take a leap of faith with my writing for a long time. I struggled with stepping out into the unknown, but I eventually chose to be like Abraham and follow the Lord's call. I wasn't sure about taking that first step, but that's where faith came into the picture.

In Genesis 12, we are reminded of how God called Abraham: *"The Lord had said to Abram, 'Leave your native country, your relatives, and your father's family, and go to the land that I will show you.'"*

Though we may never know exactly where the Lord is leading us, we can cling to the truth that He is good, and He has great plans for every single one of us.

You may have something on your heart you've felt the Lord nudging you about. Spend some time today to consider what that might be. And be reminded, as my friend did for me, sometimes we just must get up and go. (I did eventually get up and get an ice pack.)

If we choose to remain in our comfort, we may miss what God has for us there. So, I challenge you with this question: comfort vs. calling, which will you choose?

Take 5: You've stepped out in faith and started this journey. You're doing great! Take a few moments to thank Jesus for being your anchor and then ask Him to continue showing you the way—one step at a time.

STEP 2 – DISCIPLINE

I remember vividly the day I walked into my counselor's office for the first time. I was keenly aware of my surroundings—the office lighting, the way the furniture was arranged, what my counselor was wearing, and the cleanliness of the environment. I was searching for safety in what felt like a scary situation. I was hurting and wanted to heal.

Seeking counseling for my hurting heart was one of the hardest things I have ever done. I had been mustering up the courage for weeks and canceled once, but finally, the Lord gave me the strength to walk into her office. Responding to the Lord's call to action and being disciplined enough to show up that day changed my life for the better, forever.

In my job as a physical therapist, one of my primary responsibilities is to educate my patients. Once they develop a deeper understanding of their pain, they are better able to understand the courage and discipline that will be required for them to heal.

During my patients' first visit, I intentionally lay out a foundational plan. I provide specific action steps by discussing what I will do for them in the clinic, what exercises I will ask them to do at home, and what things they should avoid to protect their healing. Each of these steps is helpful individually, but when performed collectively, healing often happens much more quickly.

By laying out expectations, it helps prepare patients for any bumps they may meet along the way. As their physical therapist, it also helps me guide and encourage them as they begin to take ownership of their symptoms and choose the discipline needed to move forward in the healing process.

The same principals apply to the healing of our hurting hearts. When we're hurting and walking an extremely long journey, it can be easy to become discouraged and give up before reaching our destination.

Thankfully, God always supplies the strength and courage we need to do the challenging work of healing. The Bible affirms this truth in 2 Timothy 1:7: *"For God has not given us a spirit of fear and timidity, but of power, love, and self-discipline."*

Heart work requires us to be disciplined to continue moving forward even when we are feeling weary. Just as I give my patients specific exercises to do daily for physical healing, there are "exercises" we can do to help our hearts heal.

- Connecting to God through reading the Bible and prayer
- Seeking support from trusted friends or mentors
- Committing to professional counseling

And while each one of these is valuable on its own, there's an even greater impact on healing when we step forward in them together.

Prayer & Bible Reading

Connecting with an invisible God can sound impossible, but God wants to connect with us. The Bible is His love letter to us. It is also an instruction manual and our coaching guide. God wants us to know who He is, why He created each of us, and how we can have a full life when we choose to walk with Jesus.

As for prayer, it is a way to listen and talk to God—pausing to give Him our attention and sharing what's on our mind or stirring in our heart.

Spending a little time reading the Bible each day really helped me jump-start my journey of healing. I began to pray, pause to connect with God, and listen. Paying attention to what God was saying through His Word and in my time of prayer, my heart opened, and I began to tap into His wisdom and truth.

The same can be true for you, too. Start small. Read a verse or a short chapter each day. Start with the devotions here—each one has a verse to help center us with God's truth. Then spend a few minutes sharing with God whatever is on your heart. Thank Him, ask Him a question, or share with God what you need help with. Nothing is too big or small for God—He listens to everything that is on our hearts when we pause to connect with Him.

Whether you know the Bible well, are familiar with a few stories from going to church, or have never read the Bible, the Lord will meet you as you spend time listening and speaking to Him.

Committing to this step of prayer and connecting to God's Word is so important. It will give you the courage to stay disciplined and push forward—especially when it's difficult to see where the Lord is leading you.

Support & Mentorship

Another important part of the journey is seeking support from close, trusted friends or mentors. Just as a physical therapy patient may need to rely on a friend or family member to drive them to their appointments after a surgery, we all need people in our life to walk by our side and support us when we're hurting.

If you feel like you are walking the path alone, reach out. Check in with your local church—there are people who can help in practical ways. If you want to build relationships, find out if there are any community groups, Bible studies, or supper clubs that meet close to your house. Building relationships happens with time and consistency. The first step is yours to take.

By seeking connection points in your community, I believe the Lord will begin to surround you with supportive friends who can speak truth into your difficult circumstances, help you navigate the hard, and, ultimately, point you to Jesus. Their role isn't to fix, but their encouragement and commitment to fill in the gaps on your journey is a transformational part of the healing process.

Professional Counseling

Seeking professional counseling is another incredibly useful tool for the journey. Just like you would see a doctor when you have a fever and go to physical therapy for back pain, there are trained professionals who are ready to help you begin addressing your heart and soul pain too.

As a physical therapist, my years of training—in-depth education, understanding of the human body, and first-hand experience helping patients heal—prepared me to help patients in ways that Google cannot help.

In the same way, professional counselors can help in ways even trusted friends can't. They are trained to help diagnose the pain points of our heart and soul. And they are equipped to help us find our blind spots and to give us tools to move forward in growth.

Just as I teach my patients specific movements that will help heal and strengthen their body, professional counselors can teach us specific skills for our mind, emotions, and relationships that are often lost when we're wounded.

Through prayer, connecting to God's Word, having a difficult conversation with a close friend, and choosing to seek professional counseling, the Lord helped me move me from hurting to healing. He wants to do the same for you.

The journey isn't easy, but the Lord continually reminds me of His promise found in Galatians 6:9: *"So let's not get tired of doing what is good. At just the right time we will reap a harvest of blessing if we don't give up."*

Do not give up. Jesus will guide you and give you courage as you choose to continue moving forward. Keep taking the next step.

The next ten devotions will point you to prayer, guide you toward connecting with God's Word, and encourage you to find evidence of God's faithfulness in the everyday moments of life.

Reflection Questions

1. Think about your daily routine. Where can you carve out 10–15 minutes daily to spend time with Jesus? Write down two to three options and commit to build this life-giving habit.

2. Think about the people with whom you interact daily. Is there someone who comes to mind that you may be able to connect with regularly? Write down the names of a few friends or family members you can reach out to for support.

3. How else can you equip yourself for this journey? Write down two to three sources of accountability (a professional counselor, a local pastor, etc.). Look up their contact information and plan for how you can connect with them.

Day 11: Necessary Things

No discipline is enjoyable while it is happening—it's painful! But afterward there will be a peaceful harvest of right living for those who are trained in this way.

Hebrews 12:11

A friend and I recently chatted about her workday schedule. She works from home but partners with others on projects. Without a detailed outline of responsibilities and deadlines, it is difficult for the team to successfully meet essential client parameters. As a result, her days are consumed with five hours of online meetings. And she only has one thirty-minute break!

I was impressed by her schedule and commiserated with her. She shared how important it was that everyone on the team was on the same page about the process of completing their projects. Each person meticulously had to follow the steps outlined by the company to complete their responsibilities. This required a certain amount of discipline, and when a detail got dropped, it created a mess for everyone else.

As we discussed this concept, my mind was drawn to the verse from Hebrews 12:11: *"No discipline is enjoyable while it is happening—it's painful! But afterward there will be a peaceful harvest of right living for those who are trained in this way."*

There are many ways to apply this truth, but for me, it serves as a reminder that we often must do the necessary things—even if they aren't what we want to do—to reap a good harvest later.

In my friend's case, when each person contributing to the project uses their training and skills, it allows everyone to work together and produce a high-quality final product.

Not just with our jobs but with everything in life, we can get tired, stray from our training, and do things our own way. Though this may seem easier in the moment, it will never lead us to a place of productivity or peace. It's worth taking some time to think about what things in life we might be dropping or avoiding.

God has given us the gift of the Bible as a training manual. That doesn't mean following it is always easy. Often it requires us to change old habits or patterns and that is not easy.

However, if we commit to discipline, surround ourselves with a group of people who have different gifts, and work together toward the common goal of glorifying God, our training won't fail to produce. The harvest will far outweigh any pain we may go through during the training process.

Take a few minutes to confess to God what you've been avoiding, then ask Jesus to give you the strength to do what you know you must do—even if it requires a long meeting or two.

Take 5: Are there any things you've been avoiding? Maybe there's someone you need to apologize to and ask forgiveness. Or maybe there's a habit that's not healthy and you need to break it. Journal about whatever comes to mind, then make a plan to act on it.

Day 12: Settled in Christ

You will keep in perfect peace all who trust in you, all whose thoughts are fixed on you!

Isaiah 26:3

I once watched a University of Kentucky basketball game—my home team—where our guys looked out of sync, especially at the beginning of the game. It was a road game in a hostile environment, and the opposing team was putting a lot of pressure on us. Quite frankly, our guys didn't handle the pressure well at all.

I pulled out my phone and typed out a post (because we all know those of us sitting on our couches at home have all the right answers): "Definitely looking a little unsettled in the early minutes, but I'm confident we'll loosen up a little! Loving the packed house. #BBN."

I meant every word of the message I shared. It was not a typical performance for several of our guys. It was clear that our players were unsettled and rattled by the environment, and this affected their play. They made lots of mistakes throughout the game, partially due to pressure from the defense and partially due to poor decision-making. But our guys never gave up the fight.

As followers of Jesus, that's true for us too. We must never give up.

But there are times when we may feel unsettled—waiting for results of a medical test, dealing with never-ending home repairs, seeing someone we love deal with the outcome of some poor decisions, leaning into a dream but feeling like the Lord hasn't given us enough direction.

There are many things in this life that try to rattle our peace. It reminds me of one of my favorite verses from the Bible, Isaiah 26:3: *"You will keep in perfect peace all who trust in you, all whose thoughts are fixed on you!"*

When external pressures—difficult circumstances beyond our control or the results of poor decision-making—start to creep up and try to steal our peace, we must remind ourselves to lean on what we know is true: ultimate peace and victory are only found in Jesus.

While watching the Kentucky basketball game, despite their struggles, I saw our guys continue to lean into what they have been taught for years: the fundamentals of the game. They were playing defense, stepping up to make free throws, responding to the punch, being supportive of their teammates, and most of all, continuing to fight.

My prayer for all of us today is that when life throws a crazy pass our way and we begin feeling unsettled, we would turn to the fundamentals: read the Word of God and pray. If we can lean into the truth contained on those pages, we will find ourselves at peace as our thoughts are fixed on Him.

If you're new to the training, don't fret. Start small. Google popular scripture verses. Pick up a Bible and be curious. Talk to friends who have been following Jesus for years. Keep reading, looking for, and leaning into finding truth. Most of all, keep fighting, and you will eventually find yourself settled in Christ.

Take 5: Write down 2-3 Bible verses that focus on peace (start with today's verse) and turn to your list whenever life begins to feel unsettled. Let the fundamentals of God's truth bring you peace.

Day 13: Blind Spot Monitoring

Search me, O God, and know my heart; test me and know my anxious thoughts. Point out anything in me that offends you and lead me along the path of everlasting life.

Psalm 139:23–24

A few years ago, I upgraded to a new-to-me vehicle that I bought from my twin brother and his wife. After picking up the car, I cruised down the interstate, heading home in my new whip. I was loving all its features: SiriusXM radio, a backup camera, and heated seats just to name a few.

One feature I wasn't expecting was blind spot monitoring, a feature that detects and lets you know of vehicles in adjacent lanes. At first, I was slightly annoyed at all the flashing and beeping. After all, I had always relied on my own vision to check the blind spots. But they're called blind spots precisely because they're difficult to see.

Have you ever been in a situation on the road when you've missed something in your blind spot? I know that's true for me, on the road, and in life. At times, we are all blinded by our own perceptions and prejudices that have been born from our unique life experiences. Those blind spots don't make us bad people, but they do highlight the importance of *spiritual* blind spot monitoring.

I love that the Lord often supplies what we need through the people around us. I am so grateful to have so many trusted friends who walk beside me on this journey. Like the sensors in my car's side mirrors, these friends have become my *spiritual sensors*, alerting me when they see something I don't. And this gives me the peace of mind to keep my eyes on the road ahead.

Psalm 139: 23–24 has helped me a lot as I've grown in my walk with the Lord: *"Search me, O God, and know my heart; test me and know my anxious thoughts. Point out anything in me that offends you and lead me along the path of everlasting life."*

These verses are a prayer. I want the Lord to search my heart and show me areas of my life where I may not be seeing clearly. When I am relying on the blind spot monitoring, I can keep my eyes focused on the narrow path ahead.

Think about the relationships in your life. Do you have friends, coworkers, family members, or a spouse who acts as your blind spot monitor? If you don't have anyone who speaks into your life in this way, ask the Lord to show you who can help you when you may not see clearly.

Just like when we buy a new vehicle, when we say yes to following Jesus, we have access to new features in our lives, the greatest of which is the Holy Spirit. If we are willing to pay attention to the features, He will always be our signal and our guide.

Take 5: Ask God to reveal any blind spots that may be causing you to veer off course. Thank Him for the work He has already done in your life as you continue to move forward in healing.

Day 14: Start Small

Do not despise these small beginnings, for the Lord rejoices to see the work begin, to see the plumb line in Zerubbabel's hand.

Zechariah 4:10

It was a gloomy weekend morning, and I was feeling super lazy. I hadn't slept great the night before. My mood mirrored the weather, and I had a pretty strong case of "the blahs." I have learned that when this feeling starts to creep up, it's important for me to make myself get up and do something before that feeling makes itself at home.

Being in that spot can be difficult—I know I need to get up and do something productive, spend time with the Lord, pray, or be physically active. Sometimes the pull of the enemy is strong as he tries to keep me seated right where I am, surrounded by a cloud of whatever negative emotion I may be feeling in the moment. Perhaps you can relate.

We need to work out, but we struggle to get motivated. We need to eat healthy, but we crave sugar. We want to pray, but we don't know where to start. We want to worship, but we have trouble finding our voice. That is when we must remember to start small.

That gloomy morning, the Lord gave me the strength to do just that. I refilled my coffee and made myself start a small load of laundry. That small act helped pull me out of the funk I was stuck in that morning.

Maybe you find yourself feeling stuck today. You may be dealing with chronic pain. You may have lost your job. You may be struggling to lose the weight you need to feel better. You or someone you love may be dealing with a medical crisis. Or maybe you have no idea why you simply cannot shake the funk you're in. Emotions can feel overwhelming at times and the burden heavy. Even starting small can feel too big.

Still, doing something small can set change in motion. My decision to start with a small load of laundry led to me doing three loads of laundry, vacuuming the house, cooking breakfast, prepping a few snacks for the week— even baking an entire batch of cinnamon rolls!

What could have been a day of battling for control over my thoughts and emotions ended up being a productive day. Even better was getting to end it by sharing my home-made cinnamon rolls with people the Lord has blessed my life with. All because I asked God to give me the strength to start small.

I want to point you today to the verse from Zechariah 4:10 that tells us: *"Do not despise these small beginnings, for the Lord rejoices to see the work begin, to see the plumb line in Zerubbabel's hand."*

Whatever you're facing today, let me assure you that Jesus can take even your small efforts and do far more than you could ever hope for or imagine. Just get started.

Instead of putting off exercise, start by going for a ten-minute walk each day. Instead of avoiding a major diet change, start by cutting out one sugary food or drink. To build a habit of prayer and worship, start by turning on some worship music while you get ready for the day. And if all you can muster is a single word, sit with that word before Jesus. He will meet you in the small beginnings.

Take 5: Ask Jesus to help you start small. Write down a list of a few things that come to mind. Choose to be disciplined as you continue to take small steps forward in faith.

Day 15: Come to the Table

Later, Levi invited Jesus and his disciples to his home as dinner guests, along with many tax collectors and other disreputable sinners.

Mark 2:15

After I bought my house, I started slowly accumulating furniture, decor, and anything that would make my house a home. With a limited budget, I worked my way through the house one room at a time, focusing first on the rooms where I would be spending most of my time, including my dining room—the space where I could host friends and family.

My favorite purchase by far was the dining room table! It's a beautiful piece of furniture, and I was okay with spending a good chunk of money on it. To me, my dining room table is so much more than just a surface on which to eat. My prayer was that it would help create a space where I could invite others to gather and share a meal.

There isn't much that has played a more valuable role in my spiritual journey than gathering around the table. I am forever grateful for the friends and families who have welcomed me into their homes. Sharing a meal opened the door for us to cultivate deep relationships, learn more about ourselves, dive into connections centered around Jesus, and simply have so much fun—all the while filling our bellies.

Gathering around the table is such a simple concept, and it's something Jesus did too. He even met for a meal with those others despised. Mark 2:15 says: *"Later, Levi invited Jesus and his disciples to his home as dinner guests, along with many tax collectors and other disreputable sinners."*

Though this decision yielded scrutiny from everyone around Him, Jesus chose to eat with them anyway. When others objected, Mark 2:17 tells us that *"On hearing this, Jesus said to them, 'It is not the healthy who need a doctor, but the sick. I have not come to call the righteous, but sinners.'"*

The truth contained in these verses is so critical. When we are sick, we need a doctor. As sinners, we need a Savior—each and every one of us. Jesus invites us to the table and offers us His free gifts of grace, mercy, and unconditional love. One day, all the followers of Jesus will gather around His table. The best news of all is that *everyone* is invited.

Each time I walk through my house and pass by my dining room table, my prayer is to remember all those who have so lovingly extended the invitation to me to *come to the table*. In return, I pray I am intentionally doing that for others.

Take 5: Take a moment today and consider who might need an invitation to come to the table. Ask Jesus to lead you and thank Him for the opportunity to extend His love to others.

Day 16: Power Source

And this same God who takes care of me will supply all your needs from his glorious riches, which have been given to us in Christ Jesus.

Philippians 4:19

One afternoon at work, I had just escorted a patient to the front desk when my co-worker stopped me.

"Hey, is this laptop charger yours?" he asked.

"If it's the broken one, then yes," I hollered back.

"If it's broken, what good is it to you?"

"It might be chipped, but every time I plug it into the power source it still charges my laptop."

"Okay, cool. Can I give it a try?"

The first thing I do at work every morning is to check my laptop's battery level. I move around rooms to see patients and take my computer with me: I need it to document treatments, write letters to other doctors on behalf of patients, check email, and stay updated on schedule changes. If I don't have enough battery supply at the start of my day, my laptop won't last through the day—which creates a problem. Thank goodness we can recharge computer batteries!

The same is true in my daily life. I wake each morning knowing I need a certain amount of energy to carry out the tasks set before me that day. How much energy I wake up with depends on so many different factors—how I slept the night before, my health, the state of my relationships, work stress, and more.

We all have some things in our lives that drain our energy, while others tend to fill us up. And no matter what lies before us each day, we must enter each day with a certain level of energy to do what is asked of us. Though our days may look different, I don't know anyone who doesn't have multiple things competing for their time and energy. It can be difficult to prioritize tasks on our to-do lists and make sure we have enough energy to do the most important tasks before we run too low and shut down.

Just like my broken laptop charger still works if I plug it into a power source, so can you and me. Though we are broken and weary, the Lord can still use us if we connect back to the source, Jesus Christ.

How? Through God's Word. The Bible is our ultimate power source, which allows us to recharge our hearts, minds, and souls when we feel depleted.

Philippians 4:19 gives us this promise: *"And this same God who takes care of me will supply all your needs from his glorious riches, which have been given to us in Christ Jesus."*

So, when you're feeling worn out and drained, wondering how you will find the energy to attack the never-ending to-do list for your day, remember to recharge. Connect to the power source by spending time in God's Word.

I'm so incredibly grateful that He doesn't give up when we are chipped, that He can supply all we need to carry out the tasks He sets before us.

Take 5: Consider what you rely on to recharge daily. Ask Jesus to show you how you might connect with Him during your day and thank Him for supplying all your needs.

Day 17: A Speck in My Eye

And why worry about a speck in your friend's eye when you have a log in your own?

Matthew 7:3

After many instances of breaking my glasses while playing sports, I was pumped when I could finally switch to wearing contacts. Wearing contacts was so much easier, but it didn't come without some inconveniences.

The smallest speck would send me off the court to deal with the discomfort.

But you don't have to wear contact lenses to know the pain having something in your eye can cause. One night I suddenly had a sharp pain in my eye whenever I blinked. I found myself staring at the mirror, trying to locate the problem. Finally, I spotted it—a tiny little eyelash stuck in my eye. *How could something that small cause that much pain?* I wondered as I removed the eyelash.

At that moment, I was reminded of these words in Matthew 7: 3–5: *"And why worry about a speck in your friend's eye when you have a log in your own? How can you think of saying to your friend, 'Let me help you get rid of that speck in your eye,' when you can't see past the log in your own eye? Hypocrite! First get rid of the log in your own eye; then you will see well enough to deal with the speck in your friend's eye."*

When I pause and consider the amount of pain caused by an eyelash, it leads me to ask myself what log I might be carrying in my heart? How often do we choose to focus on getting rid of the speck in a friend's eye instead of dealing with the log in our own?

It's a heavy question if we answer it honestly, but worth exploring.

When we are working through the challenges life throws our way, it's not our ability to fix others that leads to growth and healing. Rather, it's our ability to take care of the log(s) in our own eye. When we're afraid to honestly address our own patterns, we're choosing to live with the pain.

This is why seeking formal Christian counseling has been one of the most important choices I've made. A good counselor supports us as we courageously stand in front of the mirror and look closely at the reflection staring back at us.

When we choose to walk with Jesus, He will meet us at the mirror with unconditional love. Though it may be painful, I want to encourage you to make a commitment to examine what you see in the mirror of your heart. Allow Him to heal and restore you.

Take 5: Step in front of a mirror today. Prayerfully reflect on ways Jesus is calling you to deal with the log in your own eye. Write them down and express gratitude that He is walking with you through the healing.

Day 18: Pursuit, Not Perfection

Fear of the Lord is the foundation of wisdom. Knowledge of the Holy One results in good judgment.

Proverbs 9:10

Thursdays tend to be hectic for me. On those days, my work schedule is often packed. And because it marks the end of my work week, I am usually more than ready to spend a little time winding down when I get home.

Because my job is very physical, one would think that I'd simply want to relax with an enjoyable book. That's sometimes the case, but I often prefer to unwind from a busy week at the basketball court up the street from my house. This outdoor court has become a sanctuary for me.

That was where, some time back, I spent time shooting hoops after work. I needed to quiet my mind, pray, release worries, and ultimately, just connect quietly with the Lord.

I cannot begin to count the number of jump shots I've taken in my lifetime. Even just out back at my parent's house growing up. I have invested so much time in this craft that I know what perfect form feels like. As a result, I often immediately recognize a flaw in my shot that will lead to a miss.

As I was putting up a few jumpers that Thursday afternoon, I took a shot, and immediately thought, *I had too much palm on that shot.* As I knew it would, the ball clanged off the rim and sent me on a chase to recover my miss.

Though this may seem like I focus on perfection, for me this is more about developing a thorough understanding of proper form and being able to execute consistently. And this leads to success. Perfection is not the goal but rather the continual pursuit.

As I kept shooting hoops that afternoon, I felt convicted by the Holy Spirit. I want to know the Word of God better than I know my jump shot. But, if I'm being honest, that's not the case.

Have I spent as many hours studying the Bible as I've spent perfecting my jump shot? No. Have I spent more time on a basketball court than I have with my nose inside the pages of God's Word? Yes. I don't think God wants me to choose one or the other. It should be both.

The value of all those hours of practice was the awareness I developed of my form. I can detect what's wrong because I confidently know what *feels right.*

Likewise, when we know the Word of God deeply and intimately, it develops in us the knowledge of good versus evil. Proverbs 9:10 says: *"Fear of the Lord is the foundation of wisdom. Knowledge of the Holy One results in good judgment."*

When we invest in the Word of God with the same level of commitment that we give to sports, school, work, we will begin to develop wisdom and an understanding of the Holy One that will strengthen our minds and hearts. When we intimately know what is *right,* we are more equipped to immediately recognize when something we hear or read is not founded in biblical truth. And in today's world, that will always be our best defense.

Take 5: Make an investment today. Commit to setting aside a specific amount of time to spend with Jesus each day. Remember to give yourself grace as you develop this new habit.

Day 19: Patient in Prayer

I am praying to you because I know you will answer, O God. Bend down and listen as I pray.

Psalm 17:6

I sat staring at a flashing cursor for a long while one morning. There was a stirring in my heart to write, but the words I was searching for just weren't quite there. Not yet at least. I typed a few letters, then tapped delete.

As I saw it, I had three choices: I could give up–not going to happen. As I sometimes do, I could put the laptop away and return the next morning after I rested. Or I could sit in the quiet, pray, and wait it out.

Just like so many situations in life, I want things to happen *right now.*

I want to find a new job *right now.*

I want to get rich *right now.*

I want to meet my husband *right now.*

I want this new gadget *right now.*

I want to publish a novel *right now.*

Today, instant results are often the norm. Delayed gratification seems to be a thing of the past. We don't like to wait for anything. Because of technological advancements over the last twenty years, access to information, supplies, goods, is at an all-time high.

Do you want the latest gadget or toy? Order on Amazon. It will arrive *in 1-3 days.*

Do you want to watch a new movie or TV show? Turn on Netflix any time that suits you.

Do you want food right now? Click on Door Dash and your meal arrives in thirty minutes.

Do you want a coffee to start your day? Order on the Starbucks app and they'll have it ready and waiting.

No wonder we are no longer patient. No wonder it is so hard to pause, pray, and wait while the Lord works.

Unfortunately, that has become true when it comes to jobs, relationships, houses, vehicles, and so much more. If whatever we want isn't immediately available or what we have doesn't seem to be giving us what we want at this moment, we start looking for the next best thing. Often, we just walk away.

We leave jobs when there's discord at the workplace instead of prayerfully asking the Lord if there may be a reason, He wants us to stay.

We walk away from friendships when the other person does something hurtful instead of prayerfully asking the Lord to help us extend grace and forgiveness.

We buy a house that's out of our price range instead of prayerfully asking the Lord to lead us to a home that fits our needs and our budget.

I'm not suggesting that we stay in jobs or relationships that are no longer healthy. Instead, I am suggesting that we take the time to step back, examine our struggles, and ask, *Am I being patient in prayer, and taking these difficult situations to the Lord before making a decision?*

Psalm 17:6 says: *"I am praying to you because I know you will answer, O God. Bend down and listen as I pray."*

When the *right now* doesn't come, instead of walking away, wait. Call on God. Be patient with Him in prayer, give Him a listening ear, and wait. He will guide your thoughts, words, and actions as you move forward in prayer with whatever decision you're facing.

Take 5: Write a prayer for patience. Keep it in your purse, in your wallet, or on the bathroom mirror. Recite the prayer aloud daily as you allow the Lord to guide your decisions.

Day 20: First Line of Defense

My prayer is not for the world, but for those you have given me, because they belong to you.

John 17:9

A couple of years ago, I was fascinated by the Enneagram, a personality typology designed to help us better understand the motivation behind our actions. *Disclaimer: Just like with any good tool, I believe the Enneagram can be valuable and useful, but it does not diminish, replace, or rise above the truths and promises of the Lord found in the Word of God.*

After doing a lot of reading, research, and even taking a test to see what Enneagram type I am, I discovered that I am a type 2, which is defined by some as a "Nurturing Supporter." Enneagram expert Beth McCord describes it this way: "Type 2s are people who see the world through relationships and define themselves through their service to others."

Anybody who knows me well at all can affirm that, though this definition is not all-encompassing, it does provide some quick insight into how the Lord made me. My relationships are the greatest joys of my life, and my desire to serve others has always been a primary motivator in my life.

Though my love of relationships and service to others are gifts from the Lord, they can quickly become a source of dependency, manipulation, or pride. I am grateful for how the Lord has allowed me these insights. In conjunction with Christian counseling and a dependence on biblical truth, I have learned to better understand my motivations and the root of my thoughts, words, and actions.

Jesus fully and completely loves me. I am made whole because I am a daughter of the One True King. When I remember these foundational, biblical truths, I can lean into the Holy Spirit and seek His guidance when it comes to the best way to serve and love others.

My tendency is to rescue, to help, to fix. Though my intention is wholesome, if I'm not careful, I can allow self-idolatry to replace prayer as my first line of defense when it comes to loving and serving my people.

It has taken me a long time to grasp the importance of this truth in my life. However, since doing so, my life has been forever changed for the better. When I lean into prayer as my first line of defense, I can keep my sinful tendencies in check while staying open to however the Lord may lead me to serve those I love.

John 17:9 says: *"I am praying for them. I am not praying for the world but for those whom you have given me, for they are yours."* As a follower of Jesus with a heart designed toward love of relationships and service to others, Jesus invites me to lean into prayer and remind myself that the ones I love ultimately belong to the Lord, not to me.

Though I must continually be mindful of my tendencies toward dependency and pride, I have discovered the freedom that is found in making prayer my first line of defense. And that has changed everything.

Take 5: Jot down a list of names of the most important people in your life. Ask God to give you words of prayer for each person and turn this prayer list into your first line of defense.

STEP 3 – TRUST

Trust is a choice. It develops over time, through experience, and through repeated exposure.

As a physical therapist, my first appointment with a new patient is crucial because it lays the foundation for setting up a trusting relationship. Can they trust that I will truly listen as they share their symptoms? Can I trust that they will do their part and stick with their home exercises? Will healing come, even when progress seems slow?

Because I've been at my same clinic for over ten years now, I've worked with many patients more than once. When they have a new injury, they come back to see me because experience has proven they can trust me. They are willing to trust me as I guide them.

When I tell them the pain they're experiencing is temporary, they believe me. They listen when I remind them the pain of exercise is productive and that it helps them move toward healing. And when they stay the course, it is a beautiful thing to watch them experience measurable progress toward their goals.

But when it comes to being trustworthy, Jesus is far wiser and more faithful. More than supplying physical healing, His heart is to see us healed and whole on the inside, too.

Unfortunately, we may have gone through difficult life experiences that can make it difficult to trust God's process. Some of us have had a friend disappoint us, while others have had a person at church turn their back on us. Maybe an employer lied to us, or a coach abandoned us. Hurts like these create wounds that break trust. They cause us to begin building walls that we think will protect us. In reality, these walls may keep us from moving forward.

Our protective walls often keep us from trusting Jesus too. Yet when we are willing to let Jesus guide us, He will help us through to the other side.

Jeremiah 17:7–8 gives us this promise: *But blessed are those who trust in the Lord and have made the Lord their hope and confidence. They are like trees planted along a riverbank, with roots that reach deep into the water. Such trees are not bothered by the heat or worried by long months of drought. Their leaves stay green, and they never stop producing fruit.*

With Jesus, we can begin to tear down the walls we've built around our hearts and step forward on the healing path. Here are three ways we can build that trust.

Commit to Change

Healing physical injuries often requires breaking old patterns of movement. This doesn't happen overnight. It requires commitment in the form of showing up for appointments and performing exercises at home.

The same goes for injuries to our heart and soul. When I finally decided to get serious about healing my heart, I committed to doing whatever was necessary to keep taking steps forward: I set my alarm to get up early to read my Bible and pray. I shared my struggles and successes with a close friend who walked with me as an accountability mentor. And I made regular counseling appointments and showed up for those.

No matter how hard I worked, though, this healing journey has taken time. And it will continue to take time, commitment, and prayer. But the Lord is committed to our growth. Proverbs 16:9 says, *"Commit your actions to the Lord, and your plans will succeed."*

Instead of building walls that keep us stuck in pain, we can choose to be persistent in filling our minds with God's truth while also seeking wise counsel and support. Our job is to commit our actions to God—then leave the rest up to him.

Be Mindful

I am good at ignoring the things I don't want to deal with— my nagging back pain, getting an oil change for my car, pulling weeds in my flower bed. When patients walk into my office, they've often done the same with their physical pain. They've chosen to ignore the symptoms for a long time, and when they finally come to me, I must help them listen to their body and pay attention to their symptoms.

Ignoring the pain is especially true when it comes to heart wounds. Thankfully, my counselor encouraged me to begin listening to my heart, to pay attention to the pain points that were showing up in my life.

She guided me in how to pause, ask myself some meaningful questions, and assess the wounds of my heart—questions to help me name, qualify, and recognize the depth of what I was feeling. Only then could I treat the wounds, learn God's measurements for success, and develop new skills for my relationships.

We cannot make changes to heal wounds we are not aware of or willing to acknowledge. This may have been the most difficult part of the process for me. It was hard. It hurt. But choosing to trust Jesus as I peeled back those emotional layers helped me push through the hard parts and allow God to heal me.

He wants to do the same for you.

Identify God's Faithfulness

Helping my patients chart their progress is one of my favorite parts of my job. When their pain spikes, they struggle to meet a goal, or they feel like they aren't moving forward, I remind them of how far they've come. We look at measurable changes—improvements in mobility, for example, or increased strength. By reviewing their goals and showing them the progress they've made, it helps them continue to push forward when the healing is hard.

We can chart our progress with God too. When I'm caught in the middle of something hard and I'm wrestling with confusion or chaos, I look back to find God's faithfulness and remember how far he's brought me. This helps me continue to trust Him in the process.

Perhaps Jesus has led you to an encouraging Bible verse, one that clarifies the doubt that may be weighing on your heart. Or He gives you the strength to set a healthy boundary, even when it's difficult.

Along your journey, write down the ways God shows up, big or small. When you're feeling discouraged, pull out these reminders of all the ways He is guiding you. Celebrate the small victories. Acknowledge the baby steps. Charting your progress will help you trust Him as you continue to move forward on the path to healing.

God's promise in Isaiah 43:18–19 reminds us of that truth: *"But forget all that—it is nothing compared to what I am going to do. For I am about to do something new. See, I have already begun! Do you not see it? I will make a pathway through the wilderness. I will create rivers in the dry wasteland."*

When you're on the path from hurting to healing, when you're weary and things feel heavy, the tendency is to stop or turn back. But you must go through the pain to get to the healing. It is the pain that will lead you to the Promised Land.

These next ten devotions highlight the truth that we serve a trustworthy God. Choose to trust that Jesus is your guiding light. Commit to actions of healing. And remind yourself of all the ways He is bringing you forward, step by step.

Reflection Questions

1. Are there challenges in your past that have caused you to build walls around your heart and may be making it difficult for you to trust God? Name them. Write them down and ask God to help you break down the walls and give you courage to trust Him.

2. Think about where you started and where you are now. Can you name two to three measurable changes? (E.g., is your stress level lower? Do you find you have a greater sense of peace? Have you received support from a friend or counselor?)

3. Choose a Bible verse that tells of God's promise to care for you and me. (It could be a verse quoted in this chapter, in one of the devotions, or another meaningful verse you've read.) Write it down as a reminder that God is trustworthy and that He will care for you.

Day 21: 'Til the Battle is Won

We are human, but we don't wage war as humans do. We use God's mighty weapons, not worldly weapons, to knock down the strongholds of human reasoning and to destroy false arguments. We destroy every proud obstacle that keeps people from knowing God. We capture their rebellious thoughts and teach them to obey Christ.

2 Corinthians 10:3–5

I've been a University of Kentucky sports fan my entire life. For as long as I can remember, I've "bled blue," and my level of happiness occasionally rises and falls based on the win-loss column, especially during basketball season. And, like any good UK fan, I know the fight song by heart! The last two lines are my favorite.

And we'll kick, pass, and
run, 'til the battle is won,

And we'll bring home the victory.

We all face battles at times, don't we? Maybe on the football field or the basketball court, in the classroom, or in the courtroom. As a follower of Jesus, though, I've come to understand that our greatest battles are often the ones fought on the battlefield of the mind.

The enemy attacks our minds because he knows if he can get to our thoughts, he can slowly begin to affect our actions, and ultimately, try to change our hearts.

As I've stepped out into ministry opportunities God has given me, the enemy has tried to come against my obedience by pushing my thoughts into a negative space. At times, I have found myself overwhelmed by doubt, discouraged, and wanting to quit. It has been a battle for my thoughts.

One afternoon as I was fighting that battle, I was reminded of 2 Corinthians 10:3–5, *"We are human, but we don't wage war as humans do. We use God's mighty weapons, not worldly weapons, to knock down the strongholds of human reasoning and to destroy false arguments. We destroy every proud obstacle that keeps people from knowing God. We capture their rebellious thoughts and teach them to obey Christ."*

This passage reminded me that when it comes to fighting the battles of my thoughts, the greatest weapon I have against the enemy is to take my thoughts to Christ. I did just that. Then I called an encouraging and supportive friend. Later that day, I also received an unexpected, yet timely, message of specific encouragement about something I had written. My confidence returned and I was able to push forward in one more step of obedience.

While writing may sound easier than a hard workout, the battles inside us can be just as taxing. By the time all was said and done that day, my mind, heart, and soul had been fighting a battle that left me feeling completely exhausted.

Being obedient in whatever God is calling us toward may not be easy, but it's always worth it.

The next time you find yourself in a battle of any kind, keep fighting. Take your thoughts to the Lord and then reach out to a friend or mentor. And remember that when you're on Team Jesus, His sacrifice on the cross has already won the ultimate battle.

Take 5: Worship and prayer are powerful weapons. Turn on your favorite worship song and write a prayer for strength for today. Be honest about any doubts or struggles in your mind and ask Jesus to give you wisdom and courage. Thank Him for His sacrifice that guarantees victory.

Day 22: The Gift of Pain

Each time he said, "My grace is all you need. My power works best in weakness." So now I am glad to boast about my weaknesses, so that the power of Christ can work through me. That's why I take pleasure in my weaknesses, and in the insults, hardships, persecutions, and troubles that I suffer for Christ. For when I am weak, then I am strong.

2 Corinthians 12:9-10

When I think about the word gift, so many thoughts flood my brain—memories of tearing into wrapping paper on Christmas morning, watching my friend's eyes light up as she opened a birthday present, welcoming newborn nieces and nephews home for the first time. These happy, momentous occasions are joyful and oh-so memorable.

But what happens when a gift comes in the form of pain? Although it's not as easy to endure as the joyful moments, I have found the gift of pain is often the most life-changing. These moments help me to remember the truth from 2 Corinthians 12:9: *"Each time he said, 'My grace is all you need. My power works best in weakness.' So now I am glad to boast about my weaknesses, so that the power of Christ can work through me."*

My life has been marked by many quaking events that, whether I realized it at the time or not, have shaped the person I am today. I am certain you may say the same, regardless of the number of years you've been on this earth.

What's most intriguing to me—yet the least talked about—is the understanding that our Heavenly Father knows every detail of our lives. He has a complete understanding of how each dot will connect to the next. As a mentor once described it to me, our life story is like a mosaic made up of all the moments of our lives.

Our perspective this side of heaven is small—like looking through the eye of a needle and struggling to see and understand the current season of life we're in, much less trying to grasp just how this dot could possibly be connected to something good. At times, we have to go through the weary process of pain and suffering. And as we do so, one dot connects to multiple others until we can finally get a glimpse of the beautiful image God is creating.

God has a great plan for each one of us. But the shifting and shaping of our lives by societal pressures can blur our perspective. It's much like waking up in the morning before I put on my glasses. You may know what it's like to see the world as a blur first thing every morning. While everything is blurry for me, I still know how to get from my bedroom to the bathroom. I have walked that path so often that I can trust my feet to get me where I'm going.

Wouldn't it be amazing if this were true in our daily walk with the Lord—especially when things are hard? That's why it's important to study God's Word and walk with Him. The more familiar we are with His truth, the more natural it becomes to place our trust in Jesus Christ and the victory that He secured for all of us when He died on the cross.

So, next time life is overwhelming, instead of trying to look through the eye of the needle to figure it all out, pause and consider the beautiful picture God is painting as one dot connects to another—for our good and His glory.

Take 5: Remind yourself today that Jesus was fully God and fully man. He knows your pain because He suffered, too. Write a prayer and ask Jesus to help you see how He is connecting the dots in your life. Ask Him to give you strength as you push forward toward healing.

Day 23: When We Don't Understand

For we are God's masterpiece. He has created us anew in Christ Jesus, so we can do the good things he planned for us long ago.

Ephesians 2:10

A friend of mine jokingly posted this call for help on social media. "We have officially entered the why stage," she said, referring to life with her toddler. "Any tips for our sanity and patience are much appreciated!"

As humans, we're hard wired to want to understand what's going on around us. Our innate desire to want to know why things are the way they are shows up at such an early age! We want to know why the sky is blue, why the grass is green, and why we have to go to bed.

For children with a never-ending stream of questions, we often answer with simple facts that appease them. Yet, as we grow into adulthood, simple answers don't quite seem to do the trick, especially once we begin to look at our world from a new perspective as Christ-followers.

When we ask God why things are the way they are, He usually doesn't have a quick answer to appease us. The deep questions are often more complicated. Often, we must wait for His answer—it may take hours, days, weeks, or even years–and they aren't always black and white. Sometimes, we don't understand God's response. And, painfully, His answer is often not what we wanted to hear. Or we are left waiting for an answer that never seems to come.

But when we enter a space of acknowledging we don't understand and choose to trust God anyway, *that* is where true freedom lies.

I have found this requires me to let go of old patterns and habits and choose to walk in step with the Spirit. Ephesians 2:10 reminds us: *"For we are God's masterpiece. He has created us anew in Christ Jesus, so we can do the good things he planned for us long ago."*

Paul of Tarsus, the man who wrote those words to the church in Ephesus, was a true example of the workmanship of Jesus. He traded his old nature as a persecutor of the followers of Jesus for being an apostle of Jesus—doing what God had long before prepared for him. Paul went from punishing Jesus's followers to risking his life to share the good news of Christ's death and resurrection with the world.

The transformation that occurs as we begin to live from a place of trust can be painful, difficult, and overwhelming. Yet, when we surrender and allow God to cultivate the fruits of the Spirit in our lives—love, joy, peace, patience, kindness, goodness, faithfulness, gentleness, and self-control—we too can begin experiencing the type of transformation that will leave us forever changed.

As a physical therapist by trade, I know how much work it requires to change old habits, build new muscle memory, and change your posture. Changing the posture of our hearts to being turned toward God instead of away from Him is no different. Healing from the inside out is no simple task.

We must lean into the truth that He is merciful, kind, and always good, even when our circumstances try to convince us otherwise. We were all created in Christ Jesus for good works. Open your heart to that type of transformation and trust Jesus through the process. He will see you through to the other side.

Take 5: Write down your why questions and take them to Jesus. Though you may not understand your circumstances, rest in knowing He hears the cries of your heart.

Day 24: How We Respond to the Storms of Life

Then Jesus said, "Come to me, all of you who are weary and carry heavy burdens, and I will give you rest. Take my yoke upon you. Let me teach you, because I am humble and gentle at heart, and you will find rest for your souls. For my yoke is easy to bear, and the burden I give you is light."

Matthew 11:28–30

With the changing of the seasons, my mind is drawn back to the summers of my youth. I spent hours every day playing with my twin brother, our cousin, and a neighbor. They were always my favorite days. But in Kentucky, sunny summer days can change in a moment as storms roll in and put a damper on a day of fun.

The storms of life can roll in as quickly. A cancer diagnosis, the loss of a child, a layoff, a divorce—you name it. We all experience times when the dark clouds roll in and devastate sunny days. Those types of storms knock us off our feet, take our breath, and cause us to experience fear in the face of the unknown.

As for me, I can struggle with letting go of control and trusting God, especially when the news is bad. I want to protect my people. I want to save them from any hurt or devastation the storms may bring. But in trying to do so, I often unintentionally elevate myself above God by trying to change, control, or carry things that are only meant for Him.

Matthew 11:28–30 says, *"Then Jesus said, 'Come to me, all of you who are weary and carry heavy burdens, and I will give you rest. Take my yoke upon you. Let me teach you, because I am humble and gentle at heart, and you will find rest for your souls. For my yoke is easy to bear, and the burden I give you is light.'"*

That first verse is popular, but the reminder that Jesus's burden is light is as critical for understanding the value of placing our cares upon God.

While in a boat with his friends once, Jesus slept during torrential rains and damaging winds. I so want to be like Jesus. Instead, like Jesus's friends, I usually find myself trying to fight the raging storm on my own. I fight until I am exhausted, to the point of fearing drowning in my circumstances.

Instead of proudly fighting our battles on our own, we can invite Jesus to calm the storm. It is from this place that we can learn to trust Jesus. Though the storm may not cease as quickly as we may hope for, His promises are true. He is with us in the storm, no matter how bad it is.

Let's keep God on the throne of our lives and remember that no matter our circumstances, He is the bearer of our burdens. He is our rescuer. When we remember that Jesus is facing the storm with us, we can experience rest, even amid a raging storm. He will give us His peace. Peace that transcends all understanding—this is a gift from Jesus, and it is a foundational truth from which we can live.

Though we may struggle to surrender our fight and allow Jesus to calm the storms for us, it is a choice completely worth making daily, moment to moment.

Take 5: Acknowledge any storms in your life right now. Remember that Jesus is in the boat with you. Write a prayer of praise and thank Him for being your protector.

Day 25: Good, Guiding Father

The Lord will guide you continually, giving you water when you are dry and restoring your strength. You will be like a well-watered garden, like an ever-flowing spring.

Isaiah 58:11

I bought a new iPhone just days before leaving for my first trip to Disney World. I knew the trip would provide memories that I would want to capture, especially since I'd be there with my brother's family, with my nieces.

Our trip to Florida was full of adventures. Wherever we went, my nieces would get so excited that they would dart ahead of the adults. We would call out, "Wait for us!" And then ask them to hold hands with an adult. Every time they would want to hold their daddy's hand. One of my favorite pictures from the trip is of my brother walking hand in hand with his girls.

My favorite day of the trip was our day in Magic Kingdom. My nieces were getting impatient as we navigated the long lines through security. Once we finally made it through, I vividly remember my sister-in-law saying, "Just wait until we round the corner up here. Then you'll be able to see the castle and it's amazing!" My nieces were so excited. Holding their daddy's hand, we maneuvered through the crowd toward Cinderella Castle.

And that's when I heard God speak to my heart. "Katie, hold my hand," He whispered. "Walk with me. You can only see a few steps ahead, but I can see it all. I know the path. I have a great plan for you. I am protecting you, and I promise to walk with you every step of the way. Trust me."

God invited me to trust Him as completely as my nieces trusted their daddy that day. I love their innocence and trusting hearts. In the crowded park, they could only see a few steps in front of them. Yet they trusted their daddy to lead them through whatever they might encounter to their dream destination, Cinderella Castle.

My brother is a wonderful father. He loves his girls deeply and would give his life to protect them. Yet, his love is but a grain of sand compared to the unconditional, perfect love of our Father in Heaven.

Those moments in the Magic Kingdom painted a surreal picture of my struggle in this life. I so wish I could see the bigger picture. I want to know where God is leading me. But, like my nieces, I am learning that taking my Father's hand and trusting Him to guide me through the process is all I need. Though I know my final destination, only He knows the challenges I will face on my journey to get there.

When we try to make our way through life without God, we end up lost, frustrated, and confused. Isaiah 58:11 reminds us: *"The Lord will guide you continually, giving you water when you are dry and restoring your strength. You will be like a well-watered garden, like an ever-flowing spring."*

I am thankful for a loving Father who guides me, satisfies my needs, and strengthens me for the journey—despite my stubbornness.

What is distracting you and keeping you from trusting God's plan for your life? Maybe it's a stressful job, a strained relationship, or an unexpected medical diagnosis that has led you to take matters into your own hands. Or maybe it's something new and exciting you're headed for—an invitation to try out for a sports team, a possible promotion, or a potential new relationship. Either way, it's easy to try and make your way on your own.

What if instead of trying to find our way on our own, we intentionally took hold of His hand and let Him guide us through these moments. He is there, and His hands are open, ready to receive ours.

Though I may struggle every single day, I am certain of this truth—God is a good, guiding, and loving Father. He is worthy of my trust. He is ready and able to guide you too.

Take 5: Is there a situation in your life you are trying to navigate through on your own? Ask God to take your hand a guide you. Then, write out today's verse, putting your own name in place of "you." Then read it again, reminding yourself of God's promise to guide you and care for you.

Day 26: Trusting His Strategy

The Lord directs the steps of the godly. He delights in every detail of their lives.

Psalm 37:23

From the time I was big enough to hold a ball in my hand, I have been playing sports. I the world of athletics, a lot of success boils down to the strength of your skillset. However, there's often not enough credit give to strategy. You can have an elite set of skills, but unless you understand how to navigate your opponents, you will lose.

The most successful athletes and coaches are those that maximize potential with a specific strategy. It's true with any competitive game.

Think of chess, for example. I learned how to play in middle school and was a bit overwhelmed by its complexity at first. It took time to learn the pieces and how each one was allowed to move. But understanding the game is just half of it. I had to learn to be strategic in capturing my opponent's pieces. That helped me elevate my skills and be successful at the game. In chess, strategy is crucial for winning.

While playing in a tournament in my eighth-grade year, my tendency to move too quickly exposed my queen and I fell in defeat to my opponent—my twin brother, David. David didn't beat me because he had better pieces than me. He won because he used a more effective strategy. He saw the bigger picture and moved his pieces effectively to protect himself while setting up the board for victory. That is a strategist at work.

The same principle is true in my walk with Christ. I have been strategic in order to grow spiritually: being intentional about spending time reading the Bible, for one. I have found that diving into God's Word is critical for getting to know His voice. And without knowing His voice, it is impossible for me to know what move to make next in the game of life.

But just as I moved too quickly in that chess match against David, when I allow emotion instead of the voice of the Lord to guide me, I can miss opportunities to allow Him to direct my steps.

Sometimes, though, I feel like my life isn't progressing as I believe it should. The pressure is there, both internally and externally, to make moves and push my life along to the place where the world says it should be. That is why I love Psalm 37:23: *"The Lord directs the steps of the godly. He delights in every detail of their lives."*

Jesus is the ultimate strategist. I am learning to allow Him to direct my steps and move me according to His plan.

Your story may be different from mine. Regardless of your circumstances, when you choose to move independently of the Lord's direction, you are setting yourself up to be exposed to the enemy.

Unlike a game of chess, I know in life the ultimate victory has already been won. Throughout the journey, even if we step off the narrow path, Jesus is always there to guide us back. Though it won't be easy, and we often cannot understand how God is moving, it will be worth it to pause, pray, and possess the victorious life God has for you. I promise you that.

Take 5: Imagine your life as a chess board. Make a list of the pieces (relationships, work, home). Before you make your next move, ask Jesus to guide you and trust that He will show you the next right step.

Day 27: The Right Path

Ask me and I will tell you remarkable secrets you do not know about things to come.

Jeremiah 33:3

I've always enjoyed being outdoors. There's something about being in nature and moving my body that helps me connect with the Lord. That's how I felt when I went for a hike on a beautiful, crisp fall day in Kentucky.

The day was beautiful. As my hiking companion and I wound our way through the trails, we discussed our struggles, our favorite things, our frustrations, and, as always, the desires of our hearts. It made me think of Jeremiah 33:3 which says, *"Ask me and I will tell you remarkable secrets you do not know about things to come."*

When we invite God into our conversations, we open the door for Him to reveal truths to our hearts. We might hear song lyrics that are specific to what our hearts need to hear. Maybe it's a rainbow in the sky that reminds us of His promises. Sometimes He speaks to us through others. That day, God showed up in a stack of rocks.

About midway through our hike, my friend and I landed on a tender topic I had been struggling with. It had left me questioning why God had allowed some events to happen. I also wondered what it meant for the direction He was leading me in.

As I shared my heart with my friend, we rounded a bend in the trail, and there was a beautiful stack of rocks—a cairn—intentionally placed by someone as a marker that we were on the right track.

I love how God works! Even when we're frustrated and lack understanding, He always gives us space to ask questions and express our frustrations. And He places reminders along our path.

When you read the Psalms, you'll find many places where David cried out to God in despair. They serve as a reminder that we're allowed to bring the fullness of our hearts before God. He is not afraid, and He wants us to come to Him. When I begin to question what God is doing in my life, it helps me to remember these truths:

- Even when life doesn't feel good, God *is* good.
- Even when things feel out of control, God *is* all-powerful.
- Even when we don't understand, God *is* all-knowing.
- Even when we don't feel loved, God *is* love.

Though things in my life don't always look as I wish they would, I am often amazed by how God speaks to my heart—both gently and firmly—at just the right time. Through a simple stack of rocks, He reminded me that I was on the right path. When I keep my heart open to hearing His voice, I will always have exactly what I need to stay on the right path. Even when I take a detour, God provides signs that direct me back toward the narrow path.

God loves me enough to show up in a stack of rocks. He loves you that much, too. On the days you find yourself searching and struggling to fully understand His ways, may you be reminded to call on Him, listen, and choose worship while you wait for Him to show up in ways that only He can.

Take 5: Gather a handful of rocks to create a cairn (or draw a stack of stones on a piece of paper). Using a marker or paints, write a character trait of God on each one. (E.g., good, all-powerful, all-knowing, protector, guide, faithful, love.) Stack your cairn someplace you will pass by daily as a reminder that God has a path for you.

Day 28: The Fast-Forward Function

The Lord is my strength and shield. I trust him with all my heart. He helps me, and my heart is filled with joy. I burst out in songs of thanksgiving.

Psalm 28:7

I am a nineties girl. My childhood is marked by Beanie Babies®, Backstreet Boys, and baseball. We had Walkmans to play music, and we had VCRs to play movies—which is why I know nearly every line from *Rookie of the Year* by heart, and I'm certain there is not a single episode of *Full House* that I haven't watched multiple times.

I still watch *Rookie of the Year*, especially now that it is available on Disney+. Doing so brings back so many good memories! But now, I can skip to a specific scene at the touch of a button. Skipping to my favorite scene was always a guessing game with a VCR. Now, I no longer have to hit fast-forward, stop, play, rewind, play, fast-forward again (you get the idea?) until I find the right spot.

Technology is a blessing in so many ways. It has also created a new level of impatience within us. Instead of patiently listening to the radio until our favorite song is played, we select it from a playlist. And instead of waiting a week for the next episode of a favorite TV show to air, we sit back as the next one automatically starts streaming.

I'm just as guilty as anyone else of being impatient. Not too long ago, I was watching a movie and became so invested in a couple of the characters that I couldn't wait to see how it worked out. Instead of watching the relationship develop, I hit fast-forward to the end just to make sure they ended up together. Typing that makes me laugh, but I'm willing to bet I'm not the only person who's done that before!

I wish there were a fast-forward function for life, too. When I start a new project, it would be nice to hit the fast-forward button and get an idea of how things will look a few months down the road. Each time I start a new dating adventure, a fast-forward function would be helpful so I can avoid heartache if I know things aren't going to work out anyway.

As much as I'd like to think having a fast-forward button for life would be a blessing, the Lord intentionally didn't give that option. If we could see all the steps we would have to take to go where the Lord is leading, many of us would never step out in faith to begin with.

As followers of Jesus, He asks us to have faith and trust that He knows exactly what He is doing, even when we can't see beyond the next step. Though this is not an easy task, Psalm 28:7 describes the joy that is found when we choose to allow our hearts to rest and trust in Him: *"The Lord is my strength and shield. I trust him with all my heart. He helps me, and my heart is filled with joy. I burst out in songs of thanksgiving."*

I am grateful the Lord loves us too much to give us glimpses down the road. In the meantime, I will continue to allow Him to strengthen me, shield me, and help me, all while experiencing joy and rest in Him.

Take 5: Gratitude is a terrific way to turn our hearts toward God. Take five minutes and make a list of things for which you are grateful. They might be big, like a job or an answer to a prayer. They might be small, like as sunny day, a flower in the yard, or a green light on your commute. Write down as many as you can.

Day 29: Through the Storm

Then the Lord said to Moses, "Why are you crying out to me? Tell the people to get moving!"

Exodus 14:15

Summer is my favorite season of the year. And in Kentucky, that means hot humid days, lake trips, weddings, ball games, and vacations. But my plans are always contingent upon the weather. We often have scattered thunderstorms, so it's vital to have a Plan B.

One evening, I was getting ready to drive to my niece's graduation. I checked the weather on my phone and noticed heavy rain in the direction I would be driving. Sure enough, as I pulled off the main road, I was greeted with a cluster of storm clouds. Unfortunately, there was no other route to get to my destination. I was forced to drive *through* the storm.

Isn't life sometimes that way, too? We're on our way to a great destination when a storm stirs up in our path. Maybe you took a new job that requires you to move away from the people you've always known. There's no way around that.

Or you quit your job to pursue a dream, but something halts your progress. There's no way around that. You must find a new job and reconsider what you believe God lays on your heart.

You've been saving money to buy your first home, but then the markets turn, draining nearly all your savings. There's no way around that. You must push through the storm and start saving again.

You've made plans for a dream vacation, but an unexpected medical diagnosis forces you to cancel it. There's no way around that. You must deal with the crisis.

Sometimes, we look for an alternate route that would allow us to avoid the storm but doing so could take us to a different destination entirely.

Moses was charged with leading the Israelites out of Egypt. Along their way to the Promised Land, the people of Israel faced many storms and were ready to give up. According to Exodus 14:12, they even went as far as to say: *"Didn't we tell you this would happen while we were still in Egypt? We said, 'Leave us alone! Let us be slaves to the Egyptians. It's better to be a slave in Egypt than a corpse in the wilderness!'"*

They were tired, they had lost sight of what God had brought them out of, and they didn't want to push through the storm to reach the destination God had promised them.

How often do we want to give up instead of pushing through? We get tired. We forget God's faithfulness. Like the Israelites, we find ourselves crying out in frustration.

But that was not the end of the story for Moses and the Israelites. Exodus 14:15 says: *"Then the Lord said to Moses, 'Why are you crying out to me? Tell the people to get moving!'"*

I love this verse because it serves as a reminder that while it's perfectly okay to cry out to the Lord in our distress from the storm, it's imperative that we choose to move forward in trust.

Like the weather in Kentucky, the storms of life can be very unpredictable. May we choose to stay calm, trust the Lord, and keep pushing through the storm.

(If you don't know the full story of how Moses and the Israelites moved forward, keep reading in Exodus to see how the Lord paved the way.)

Take 5: Write a prayer of trust today, telling Jesus about the storm you are facing. Trust that He will stay with you through the storm.

Day 30: Connecting with God

If you look for me wholeheartedly, you will find me.

Jeremiah 29:13

Do you ever feel like you're constantly looking for something? Car keys. A matching pair of socks. Your child's favorite toy. Your phone.

If you're anything like me, these moments often occur when I'm already stressed out and pressed for time. That makes it even more difficult to find the items—even when they're right where we always leave them! When we're overloaded with stress, we can even miss the phone that we're carrying in the nook of our arm.

But it's even harder when we're searching for something that isn't quite so tangible. Peace. Identity. Calm in the middle of a storm. God himself.

When the future is unknown and circumstances are out of control, life feels unpredictable and scary. It's precisely during those times when we need God the most—yet the stress can keep us from slowing down long enough to connect with Him.

One of the biggest lessons God has taught me is the importance of being intentional to connect with Him. Making church a priority is one way I do this. But God doesn't only show up there.

For me, being outside with a basketball and a hoop is one of the spaces I find myself connecting best with Jesus. This has always been a sanctified place for me. So, when I feel unsettled—often on Sunday afternoons or evenings—I pause, grab my basketball, and walk the half a mile up the street to the court where I like to play. I talk to the Lord while I shoo and then I listen. On that basketball court is where I connect with God and feel Him speak to me in ways He doesn't otherwise.

One such afternoon, amid the echoing of the ball pounding the pavement, I quietly told God, *I get it, Lord. You've always been here.* Years later, God showed me how often He has met me on that court and the one at my parents' home.

I've spent countless hours playing ball, training, but also escaping. It wasn't until that day, years later, I realized how often God had been meeting me on that court. Through all years and challenges, God was with me. He was protecting me, encouraging me, and loving me even when I was oblivious to His presence. What an amazing gift.

I love Jeremiah 29:13: *"If you look for me wholeheartedly, you will find me."*

When we slow down, temporarily release the things that are weighing us down, and become intentional about connecting with Him, the search for God's presence and evidence of His delight in us becomes a little simpler.

What does it look like for you to wholeheartedly look for Jesus? Where do you connect best with Him? Maybe it's walking through the forest. Or taking a run. Or perhaps it's sitting in your favorite chair in the quiet of the morning. The beauty is in the uniqueness of what that specific space looks like for each of us. Though it may change throughout the various stages of our lives, we must continue to be intentional to make space to connect with God.

Be intentional. Look for Him with your whole heart and I promise, He is already there waiting for you.

Take 5: If you don't have a regular time and space where you connect with God, take this time to think of a time and place you can.

HEALING - A NEW BEGINNING

Healing is a process. It's a continual loop that repeats itself as we allow Jesus to heal one area, and then a new spot of tenderness stirs in our hearts. Through the process Jesus is faithful to mold and shape us into the version of ourselves that looks most like Him.

Despite your past, despite where you've been, no matter how badly you've messed up, or how many times you've been hurt, I can promise you one thing—this process of healing is for everyone.

Our hurts are unique to our own perspectives and experiences. Some are external, caused by situations outside of our control. Others may be self-inflicted as we choose to ignore the symptoms we're experiencing because of a particular pattern of struggle.

But we don't have to allow ourselves to be defined by these hurts. We have another choice. We can choose to look to Jesus for hope. We can choose to practice discipline and look to Him each day. And we can build our trust that He wants to heal us as we identify all the ways, big and small, He shows up in the everyday moments of our lives.

Now, just like I tell my patients whose physical wounds are in the process of healing, it is important that we do not "pick the scabs," opening wounds that God has been working to heal. While wounds are healing, they can be painful, itchy, and get easily irritated. If we aren't intentional to protect them, they get bumped, the pain shoots up again, and we take steps backward in the healing process.

But protecting our wounds is just part of the process. Just like I tell my patients, we also must be diligent to do the exercise that can help us build our strength. We have to be patient with the process, allow ourselves to rest, and ease back into our activities. This isn't always easy, even when we have a visible wound to protect.

In 2018, after struggling with all kinds of symptoms for years, I had a series of doctor visits that resulted in needing surgery. I was certainly not looking forward to the surgery, but I was excited about the prospect of the healing that would come.

After the surgery, I was sent home with layers of protection—butterfly stitches and plenty of bandages. As time passed, I was slowly able to remove the layers. The incisions healed, and eventually all I had left was a scar.

I still have those scars, but they have faded and are no longer tender. They no longer keep me from living a full life, and they serve as a reminder of how far I've come because I said yes to walking through the pain to receive healing.

The same wisdom applies to your journey of healing our hearts. It takes time. We may seek counseling, form new habits, and start feeling better.

But when something triggers a painful memory or we find ourselves in an unhealthy relationship, the old symptoms may start popping up. Pain may shoot through our hearts yet again. We may be tempted to pick the scab. Don't do it. Instead, lean into the Lord and step back onto the healing path.

As long as we are living and breathing, we are constantly exposed to the potential for injury. As one wound heals, we end up with another. And, more often than not, we're dealing with more than one source of pain at the same time. But the Lord is faithful.

The Bible tells us Jesus came to heal the sick. In fact, one of the Hebrew names for God is *Iatros*, which means physician. While He walked on the earth, Jesus healed the blind, lame, and sick. But more than that, He came to heal our hearts and souls. Long before Jesus came, the writer of Psalm 147 told us Jesus would do this when he said in verse 3: *"He heals the brokenhearted and bandages their wounds."*

I have experienced this healing Jesus offers. At first, the journey was scary and full of unknowns. It was a process that began with identifying my pain points and inviting Jesus to heal my wounds—not just a temporary relief, but a deep healing.

God continues to work in my life to heal my heart and soul through prayer, Bible reading, trusted friends, and the help of a professional counselor. By the grace of God, I have been learning not to pick at emotional scabs. No matter how often I am wounded, I choose to continue taking the steps of hope, discipline, and trust, allowing Jesus to heal me.

May this be true for you as well. As you come to the end of this book, remember that it is not the end of your journey. It is just the beginning.

I encourage you to continue on your healing path, being mindful of symptoms showing up. When they do, turn to Jesus as your hope. Lean into discipline to do the hard work. And trust Jesus with your hurting heart.

From time to time, pause to look back and celebrate the ways in which Jesus has been with you every single step of this journey. It will give you the courage to continue this path of healing, and your faith will grow deeper—the marker of healing.

As your faith grows deeper, I pray you will experience an abundance of life. More joy. More peace. More gratitude. More love. More of Jesus.

That is my prayer for you.

Reflection Questions

1. How has Jesus changed your heart and helped you form new habits on your path toward healing? (Maybe it's a renewed commitment to studying God's Word. It could be that you notice yourself feeling more emotionally stable, experiencing more peace than ever before.) Write down two to three tangible ways the Lord has grown your heart during this journey.

2. What are some of your old patterns that can serve as warning signals for an unaddressed heart wound that may need some attention? Think about two or three things that tend to rise up in your life when you're struggling. (Maybe it's unprovoked anger. It could be less patience with your kids, or frustration with a co-worker.) Jot them down so you can be mindful when they show up.

3. Start a gratitude list and write down as many things as you can think of. Add to it as often as you think of something new. Use this to help you see the ways God is showing up for you along your healing path.

THANK YOU

BEFORE YOU GO, I'd like to say "thank you" again for buying this guide on how to cross the bridge from hurting to healing. I know you could have picked from dozens of books, but you chose this one. My prayer is this book has been a blessing to your life.

Now I'd like to ask for a *small* favor. Could you please take a minute or two and leave a brief review for this book on Amazon? There is no greater way to thank me than this!

Think of it as a testimony to other believers about how this book helped you and could benefit them. You can help me help others.

And if you loved it, then please let me know that too! :>

BONUS CONTENT

If you would like to dig deeper through this journey, I've created a companion resource to help you. You can download your free *The Healing Path Journal* by going to katiefiliatreau.com.

Just like I walk my patients through their physical healing—from assessing their pain to tracking their progress—this journal will give you a template to help you on your heart healing journey.

You'll find reflection questions plus more exercises to help you find your pain points and track the ways God shows up for you along your journey.

Go to katiefiliatreau.com to download your free copy.

ACKNOWLEDGMENTS

Bringing this book to life has been an amazing journey of its own. I couldn't have done it without a community of support. Thank you...

To my family, for loving and supporting me through all my endeavors. You've made sacrifices throughout my life so that I could pursue all that God has called me to and I'm forever indebted.

To my nieces and nephews, for inspiring me and filling my heart with so much joy. I love each of you so very much.

To my friends, for being my biggest cheerleaders and always pushing me forward in Jesus. Your support gives me the courage to step out wherever the Lord is leading.

To my amazing editors, Tara, and Lee. Thank you for investing in me, encouraging me, and most of all, for your friendship. It's been an amazing ride, and I'm so thankful you chose to buckle up and take it with me.

To my publisher, Dan. I am grateful that you chose to believe in this project, and most of all, in me. Your ability was invaluable, and our shared love of Jesus has no doubt pushed this project forward.

To my longtime co-worker and friend, Matt. Thank you for your kindness, laughter, and for walking the healing path alongside me. You've seen me through my most difficult days and never once strayed in your support.

To my friend, Jon, for your amazing leadership, support, and encouragement on my spiritual journey. Thank you for being a reflection of Jesus.

To Mark, a longtime neighbor who shared his gift of photography to supply the beautiful photos found in this book.

To all my past, present, and future patients in physical therapy. Forging relationships and walking with you on your journey of physical healing has continually encouraged me to pursue being the best version of myself.

NOTES

Hurting

Mental Health Statistics from the CDC: "Products - Data Briefs - Number 419 - October 2021." Centers for Disease Control and Prevention. Centers for Disease Control and Prevention, July 29, 2021. www.cdc.gov/nchs/products/databriefs/db419.htm.

APA.org Psychology Referrals: "Demand for Mental Health Treatment Continues to Increase, Say Psychologists." American Psychological Association. American Psychological Association, October 21, 2021. www.apa.org/news/press/releases/2021/10/mental-health-treatment-demand.

Discipline

Enneagram Reference: "Enneagram Type Two: The Supportive Advisor: Your Enneagram Coach." Enneagram Type Two | The Supportive Advisor | Your Enneagram Coach. Accessed June 24, 2022. www.yourenneagramcoach.com/type2.

Trust

University of Kentucky fight song: "History and Traditions," University of Kentucky, accessed December 22, 2022, https://www.uky.edu/traditions/.

Stacked Rocks Meaning: Musambi, Written by Erick. "What Do Stacked Rocks on a Trail Mean?" Trail and Summit, September 2020. https://trailandsummit.com/what-do-stacked-rocks-on-a-trail-mean/.

Healing

Iatros: O'Reilly, Karen. "Iatros-Physician & Powerful Bible Verses for Healing." Scriptural Grace, October 27, 2022. www.scripturalgrace.com/post/iatros-physician-biblical-meaning-praying-the-names-of-god-scriptures-on-healing.

Iatros Meaning: "Iatros Meaning in Bible - New Testament Greek Lexicon - New American Standard." biblestudytools.com. Accessed November 4, 2022. https://www.biblestudytools.com/lexicons/greek/nas/iatros.html.

ABOUT THE AUTHOR

Katie Filiatreau is a passionate physical therapist, writer, speaker, and youth sports coach. She earned her doctorate degree in Physical Therapy from The University of Kentucky and has worked as a physical therapist for more than 10 years.

Katie is the only girl of four siblings and was raised in a small Kentucky town. She decided to pursue physical therapy after her older brother was seriously injured in an ATV accident while she was in high school.

Her writing career began with the creation of her blog, *The Narrow Path*, in 2017. She has compiled over one hundred written devotions, which she shares weekly on her blog.

Katie is enthusiastic about showing others the love of Jesus and sharing how Jesus shows up in her everyday life. As someone who has experienced significant and transformational healing, Katie's desire is that her words will inspire others to walk a similar journey. Connect with her online at katiefiliatreau.com.